Selected Poems

IAIN CRICHTON SMITH

Selected Poems

First published in 1985 by
Carcanet Press Limited
208-212 Corn Exchange Buildings
Manchester M4 3BQ

British Library Cataloguing in Publication Data
Smith, Iain Crichton
Selected poems.
I. Title
821'.914   PR6005.R58

ISBN 0-85635-597-6

The publisher acknowledges the financial assistance
of the Arts Council of Great Britain.

Typeset by Bryan Williamson, Swinton, Berwickshire
Printed in England by SRP Ltd, Exeter

Contents

Poem of Lewis

Here they have no time for the fine graces
of poetry, unless it freely grows
in deep compulsion, like water in the well,
woven into the texture of the soil
in a strong pattern. They have no rhymes
to tailor the material of thought
and snap the thread quickly on the tooth.
One would have thought that this black north
was used to lightning, crossing the sky like fish
swift in their element. One would have thought
the barren rock would give a value to
the bursting flower. The two extremes,
mourning and gaiety, meet like north and south
in the one breast, milked by knuckled time,
till dryness spreads across each ageing bone.
They have no place for the fine graces
of poetry. The great forgiving spirit of the word
fanning its rainbow wing, like a shot bird
falls from the windy sky. The sea heaves
in visionless anger over the cramped graves
and the early daffodil, purer than a soul,
is gathered into the terrible mouth of the gale.

Aberdeen

Mica glittered from the white stone.
Town of the pure crystal,
I learnt Latin in your sparkling cage,
I loved your brilliant streets.

Places that have been good to us we love.
The rest we are resigned to.
The fishermen hung shining in their yellow
among university bells.

Green lawns and clinging ivy. Mediaeval
your comfortable lectures, your calm grammar.
The plate glass windows showed their necklaces
like writhing North Sea fish.

Nothing will die, even the lies we learn!
Union Street was an arrow
debouching on the crooked lanes, where women
sweated like leaking walls.

Statement by a Responsible Spinster

It was my own kindness brought me here
to an eventless room, bare of ornament.
This is the threshold charity carried me over.
I live here slowly in a permanent

but clement weather. It will do for ever.
A barren bulb creates my firmament.
A sister cries: "I might have learned to wear
sardonic jewellery and the lineament

of a fine beauty, fateful and austere.
I might have trained my perilous armament
on the learned and ferocious. A lover
would have emerged uniquely from that element."

I know that for a lie, product of fever.
This is my beginning. Justice meant
that a man or woman who succumbs to fear
should not be married to good merriment.

I inspect justice through a queer air.
Indeed he lacks significant ornament.
Nevertheless he does not laugh or suffer
though, like pity's cruelty, he too is permanent.

And since I was trapped by pity and the clever
duplicities of age, my last emolument
returns, thus late, its flat incurious stare
on my ambiguous love, my only monument.

Luss Village

Such walls, like honey, and the old are happy
in morphean air like gold-fish in a bowl.
Ripe roses trail their margins down a sleepy
mediaeval treatise on the slumbering soul.

And even the water, fabulously silent,
has no salt tales to tell us, nor makes jokes
about the yokel mountains, huge and patient,
that will not court her but read shadowy books.

A world so long departed! In the churchyard
the tilted tombs still gossip, and the leaves
of stony testaments are read by Richard,
Jean and Carol, pert among the sheaves

of unscythed shadows, while the noon day hums
with bees and water and the ghosts of psalms.

For the Unknown Seamen
of the 1939-45 War
Buried in Iona Churchyard

One would like to be able to write something for them
not for the sake of the writing but because
a man should be named in dying as well as living,
in drowning as well as on death-bed, and because
the brain being brain must try to establish laws.

Yet these events are not amenable
to any discipline that we can impose
and are not in the end even imaginable.
What happened was simply this, bad luck for those
who have lain here twelve years in a changing pose.

These things happen and there's no explaining
and to call them 'chosen' might abuse a word.
It is better also not to assume a mourning,
moaning stance. These may well have concurred
in whatever suddenly struck them through the absurd

or maybe meaningful. One simply doesn't
know enough, or understand what came
out of the altering weather in a fashioned
descriptive phrase that was common to each name,
or may have surrounded each like a dear frame.

Best not to make much of it and leave these seamen
in the equally altering acre they now have
inherited from strangers though yet human.
They fell from sea to earth, from grave to grave,
and, griefless now, taught others how to grieve.

Old Woman

And she, being old, fed from a mashed plate
as an old mare might droop across a fence
to the dull pastures of its ignorance.
Her husband held her upright while he prayed

to God who is all-forgiving to send down
some angel somewhere who might land perhaps
in his foreign wings among the gradual crops.
She munched, half dead, blindly searching the spoon.

Outside, the grass was raging. There I sat
imprisoned in my pity and my shame
that men and women having suffered time
should sit in such a place, in such a state

and wished to be away, yes, to be far away
with athletes, heroes, Greeks or Roman men
who pushed their bitter spears into a vein
and would not spend an hour with such decay.

"Pray God," he said, "we ask you, God," he said.
The bowed back was quiet. I saw the teeth
tighten their grip around a delicate death.
And nothing moved within the knotted head

but only a few poor veins as one might see
vague wishless seaweed floating on a tide
of all the salty waters where had died
too many waves to mark two more or three.

Sunday Morning Walk

Sunday of wrangling bells — and salt in the air —
I passed the tall black men and their women walking
over the tight-locked streets which were all on fire
with summer ascendant. The seas were talking and talking

as I took my way to the wood where the river ran quiet.
The grass lay windowed in sunlight, the leaves were raging
in furious dying green. The road turned right
round the upstanding castle whose stone, unaging,

marks how a world remains as I, being now
pack of a wandering flesh, take holiday, strolling
far from the churches' declaiming. Health will allow
riots of naiads and nymphs, so wantonly rolling

with me in leaves in woods, thinking how once
Jove took his pleasure of Leda or — splendid embracing —
god would mate with a goddess — rapid the pounce,
fruitful the hot-thighed meeting, no need for unlacing.

And occupied thus, I came where a dead sheep lay
close to a fence, days gone. The flies were hissing and buzzing
out of the boiling eyes, wide open as day.
I stood in the sunlight beside it, watching and musing.

Three crows famished yards off. Live sheep grazed far
from the rotting carcass. The jaw, well-shaved, lay slackly
there on the warm quiet grass. The household air
was busy with buzzing like fever. How quickly, how quickly

the wool was peeled from the back! How still was the flesh!
How the visiting flies would not knock at the door of the sockets!
How the hole in the side gaped red, a well-sized gash!
How the clear young lambs grazed in the shade of the thickets!

And the sun blazed hot on my shoulder. Here was no shade.
But the sheep was quiet, so quiet. There was nothing to notice
but the grape-bunched flies and the crows. Could a world have
    stayed
if I'd taken a stick in my hand to beat off the flies!

They would merely return when I'd gone and busy as always
inhabit this larder again no matter how brightly
I struck with my smart sharp stick. All I could praise —
yes, all I could praise — was the sheep lying there so quietly

not knowing, not knowing. High summer was raging around.
I stood in my slack clean clothes. The stones were burning.
The flies in the wound continued their occupied sound
as I turned my back on a death of no weeping or mourning.

By Ferry to the Island

We crossed by ferry to the bare island
where sheep and cows stared coldly through the wind —
the sea behind us with its silver water,
the silent ferryman standing in the stern
clutching his coat about him like old iron.

We landed from the ferry and went inland
past a small church down to the winding shore
where a white seagull fallen from the failing
chill and ancient daylight lay so pure
and softly breasted that it made more dear

the lesser white around us. There we sat,
sheltered by a rock beside the sea.
Someone made coffee, someone played the fool
in a high rising voice for two hours.
The sea's language was more grave and harsh.

And one sat there whose dress was white and cool.
The fool sparkled his wit that she might hear
new diamonds turning on her naked finger.
What might the sea think or the dull sheep
lifting its head through heavy Sunday sleep?

And later, going home, a moon rising
at the end of a cart-track, minimum of red,
the wind being dark, imperfect cows staring
out of their half-intelligence, and a plough
lying on its side in the cold, raw

naked twilight, there began to move
slowly, like heavy water, in the heart
the image of the gull and of that dress,
both being white and out of the darkness rising
the moon ahead of us with its rusty ring.

A Young Highland Girl
Studying Poetry

Poetry drives its lines into her forehead
like an angled plough across a bare field.
I've seen her kind before, of the live and dead
who bore humped creels when the beating winds were wild.

Nor did they know much poetry but were skilful
at healing children, bringing lambs to birth.
The earth they lived from did not make them soulful.
The foreign rose abated at their mouth.

Yet they were dancers too and feared the season
when "pale Orion shook the seas with fire."
Peculiar waters had their inner reasons
for curing wastrels of a mental star.

And she — like them — should grow along these valleys
bearing bright children, being kind to love.
Simple affection needs no complex solace
nor quieter minds abstractions of the grave.

For most must walk though some by natural flying
learn from the bitter winds a kind of praise.
These fruits are different. She will know one dying
but he by many deaths will bless her days.

Home

To have to stay
in spite of scorn, hatred,
in spite of shattered
illusions also. To be unable
to break cleanly away
since this is truly home
simple, imperishable,
since otherwhere is chill,
dull-breasted, dumb.

Since this too is hated,
loved, willed to be perfect, willed
to a finer yield,
fiercer, less barren, richer,
its harvests be completed.
Since to have seen tall men
moving in light and fire
yet human too is more
grace than can be given

this (one says) is tragic
(to be fixed on a wheel
implacable, internal,
as tears break, as roses
bowed gravely down to rock
proliferate endless versions)
is not tragic but cause
of fresh honours, horses
impelled by used reins.

Old Woman

Your thorned back
heavily under the creel
you steadily stamped the rising daffodil.

Your set mouth
forgives no-one, not even God's justice
perpetually drowning law with grace.

Your cold eyes
watched your drunken husband come
unsteadily from Sodom home.

Your grained hands
dandled full and sinful cradles.
You built for your children stone walls.

Your yellow hair
burned slowly in a scarf of grey
wildly falling like the mountain spray.

Finally, you're alone
among the unforgiving brass,
the slow silences, the sinful glass.

Who never learned,
not even aging, to forgive
our poor journey and our common grave,

while the free daffodils
wave in the valley and on the hills
the deer look down with their instinctive skills,

and the huge seas
in which your brothers drowned sing slow
over the headland and the peevish crow.

Two Girls Singing

It neither was the words nor yet the tune.
Any tune would have done and any words.
Any listener or no listener at all.

As nightingales in rocks or a child crooning
in its own world of strange awakening
or larks for no reason but themselves.

So on the bus through late November running
by yellow lights tormented, darkness falling,
the two girls sang for miles and miles together

and it wasn't the words or tune. It was the singing.
It was the human sweetness in that yellow,
the unpredicted voices of our kind.

Lenin

In a chair of iron
sits coldly my image of Lenin,
that troubling man
"who never read a book for pleasure alone."

The germ inside the sealed train
emerged, spread in wind and rain
into new minds in revolution
seeming more real than had been,

for instance, Dostoevsky. No, I can
romanticise no more that "head of iron,"
"the thought and will unalterably one,"
"the word-doer," "thunderer," "the stone

rolling through clouds." Simple to condemn
the unsymmetrical, simple to condone
that which oneself is not. By admiration
purge one's envy of unadult iron

when the true dialectic is to turn
in the infinitely complex, like a chain
we steadily burn through, steadily forge and burn
not to be dismissed in any poem

by admiration for the ruthless man
nor for the saint but for the moving on
into the endlessly various, real, human,
world which is no new era, shining dawn.

At the Firth of Lorne

In the cold orange light we stared across
to Mull and Kerrera and far Tiree.
A setting sun emblazoned your bright knee
to a brilliant gold to match your hair's gold poise.

Nothing had changed: the world was as it was
a million years ago. The slaty stone
slept in its tinged and aboriginal iron.
The sky might flower a little, and the grass

perpetuate its sheep. But from the sea
the bare bleak islands rose, beyond the few
uneasy witticisms we let pursue
their desolate silences. There was no tree

nor other witness to the looks we gave
each other there, inhuman as if tolled
by some huge bell of iron and of gold,
I no great Adam and you no bright Eve.

The Law and the Grace

It's law they ask of me and not grace.
"Conform," they say, "your works are not enough.
Be what we say you should be," even if
graceful hypocrisy obscures my face.

"We know no angels. If you say you do
that's blasphemy and devilry." Yet I have
known some bright angels, of spontaneous love.
Should I deny them, be to falsehood true,

21

the squeeze of law which has invented torture
to bring the grace to a malignant head?
Do you want me, angels, to be wholly dead?
Do you need, black devils, steadfastly to cure

life of itself? And you to stand beside
the stone you set on me? No, I have angels. Mine
are free and perfect. They have no design
on anyone else, but only on my pride,

my insufficiency, imperfect works.
They often leave me but they sometimes come
to judge me to the core, till I am dumb.
Is this not law enough, you patriarchs?

Hume

More than this I do not love you,
Hume of the reasonable mind.
There was an otter crossed the sound,
a salmon in his cold teeth.

The mist came down. Between two capes
there was no road. There was a French
salon, an adoring wench.
He picked the salmon with his teeth.

Delicate Hume who swims through all
the daring firths of broken Scotland,
there were no roads across the land.
The causes, like old fences, yawned

gravely over wit and port.
Diplomacies are what displace
the inner law, the inner grace,
the Corrievreckan of bad art.

Envoi

Remember me when you come into your kingdom.
Remember me, beggar of mirrors, when you are confirmed
in the sleep of fulfilment on the white pillow.

Remember me who knock at the window,
who hirple on my collapsing stick, and know
the quivering northern lights of nerves.

Remember me in your good autumn.
I in my plates of frost go
among the falling crockery of hills,

stones, plains, all falling and falling.
In my winter of the sick glass remember
me in your autumn, in your good sleep.

Deer on the High Hills —
A Meditation

I

A deer looks through you to the other side,
and what it is and sees is an inhuman pride.

II

Yesterday three deer stood at the roadside.
It was icy January and there they were
like debutantes on a smooth ballroom floor.

They stared at us out of that French
arrogant atmosphere, like Louis the Sixteenth
sustained in twilight on a marble plinth.

They wore the inhuman look of aristocrats
before a revolution comes, and the people
blaspheme the holy bells in the high steeple.

Before the ice breaks, and heroes in spring
come up like trees with bursting wrongs in their arms
and feed the nobles to the uniform worms.

So were these deer, balanced on delicate logic,
till suddenly they broke from us and went
outraged and sniffing into the dark wind.

Difficult to say where they go to
in the harsh weather when the mountains stand
like judging elders, tall on either hand.

Except that they know the ice is breaking now.
They take to the hills pursued by darkness and lie
beneath the starry metaphysical sky.

Sometimes in savage winter they'll come down
and beg like fallen nobles for their bread.
They'd rather live in poverty than be dead.

Nevertheless there's something dangerous
in a deer's head. He might suddenly open your belly
with his bitter antlers to the barren sky.

Especially in winter when tormented
by loneliness they descend to this road
with great bounding leaps like the mind of God.

In summer they can be ignored. They crop so gently
among the hills that no-one notices
their happy heads sunk in the feeding cresses.

But beware of them now when ice is on the ground.
A beggared noble can conceal a sword
next to his skin for the aimless and abhorred

tyrants who cannot dance but throw stones,
tyrants who can crack the finest bones:
tyrants who do not wear but break most ancient crowns.

III

One would be finished with these practical things
in order to return as deer do
to the tall mountain springs.

Nevertheless one should not so return
till soldier of the practical or doer
one wholly learns to learn

a real contempt, a fine hard-won disdain
for these possessions, marbles of unripe children,
as, again,

a deer might walk along a sweating street
stare in a cramped window and then go
back to the hills but not on ignorant feet.

IV

Forget these purple evenings and these poems
that solved all or took for myth
the pointed sail of Ulysses enigmatic.

There was Hector with his child in his arms.
Where is that other Hector
who wore the internal shield, the inner sword?

Ulysses scurries, like a rat trapped in a maze.
He wears the sharp look of a business magnate.
Late from the office he had a good excuse.

Ideas clash on the mountain tops.
By the appalled peaks the deer roar.
Simply a question of rutting, these cloudy systems

or as yesterday we saw a black cloud
become the expression of a tall mountain.
And that was death, the undertaker, present.

And all became like it for that moment,
assumption of anguish, and the hollow waters
the metaphysics of an empty country

deranged, deranged, a land of rain and stones,
of stones and rain, of the huge barbarous bones,
plucked like a loutish harp their harmonies.

V

You must build from the rain and stones,
from the incurable numbers: the grasses
innumerable on the many hills.

Not to geometry or algebra,
or an inhuman music, but
in the hollow roar of the waterfall,

you must build from there and not be
circumvented by sunlight or a taste of love
or intuitions from the sky above

the deadly rock. Or even history,
Prince Charles in a gay Highland shawl,
or mystery in a black Highland coffin.

You must build from the rain and stones
till you can make
a stylish deer on the high hills,
and let its leaps be unpredictable!

VI

Duncan Ban McIntyre, the poet,
knew them intimately, was one of them.
They had waxen hides, they were delicate dancers.

They evolved their own music which became
his music: they elected him
their poet laureate.

It was a kind of Eden these days
with something Cretan in his eulogy.
Nevertheless he shot them also.

Like shooting an image or a vivid grace.
Brutality and beauty danced together
in a silver air, incorruptible.

And the clean shot did not disturb his poems.
Nor did the deer kneel in a pool of tears.
The stakes were indeed high in that game.

And the rocks did not weep with sentiment.
They were simply there: the deer were simply there.
The witty gun blazed from his knowing hand.

VII

What is the knowledge of the deer?
Is there a philosophy of the hills?
Do their heads peer into the live stars?

Do rumours of death disturb them? They do not live
by local churchyards, hotels or schools.
They inhabit wild systems.

Do they outface winds or lie down
in warm places? Winter, interrogant,
displaces spring and summer, undulant.

Their horns have locked in blood. Yes, their horns
have gored bellies. The dainty hind
has absolute passion, similar and proud.

It is not evil makes the horns bright
but a running natural lustre. The blood
is natural wounding. Metaphoric sword

is not their weapon, but an honest thrust.
Nor does the moon affect their coupling, nor
remonstrant gods schoolmaster their woods.

Evil not intentional, but desire
disturbs to battle. The great spring is how
these savage captains tear to indigo

the fiery guts. Evil's more complex, is
a languaged metaphor, like the mists that scarf
the deadly hind and her bewildered calf.

VIII

Supposing God had a branched head like this
considering Himself in a pool.
It is not the image of the beautiful

makes it so, simply as in a mirror,
but in its fadingness, as on the ice
the deer might suddenly slip, go suddenly under,

their balance being precarious. It is this,
that makes her beautiful, she who now obscures
unconscious heavens with her conscious ray,

is concourse of bright flesh, sad, is remembering
herself so going, so implacable,
her failing voyages to the obstinate rocks:

as deer so stand, precarious, of a style,
half-here, half-there, a half-way lustre breaking
a wise dawn in a chained ocean far.

As dear, so dear, Vesuvius, rocket, you
being ice and water, winter and summer, take
the mountainous seas into your small logic.

God may not be beautiful, but you
suffer a local wound. You bleed to death
from all that's best, your active anima.

The deer and you may well be beautiful,
for through your bones as through a mathematics
concordant honouring beauty richly breaks.

IX

Deer on the high peaks, calling, calling,
you speak of love, love of the mind and body.
Your absolute heads populate the hills

like daring thoughts, half-in, half-out this world,
as a lake might open, and a god peer
into a room where failing darkness glows.

Deer on the high peaks, there have been heads
as proud as yours, destructive, ominous,
of an impetuous language, measureless.

Heads like yours, so scrutinous and still,
yet venomed too with the helpless thrust of spring,
so magisterial, violent, yet composed:

heads of a thirsty intellect, sensuous as
the thirst of bellies in a summer day
July and waspish, on a murmuring ground.

Heads like valleys where the stars fed,
unknown and magical, strange and unassuaged,
the harmonies humming in a green place.

So proud these heads, original, distinct,
they made an air imperial around
their pointed scrutiny, passionate with power.

Electric instinct of the high hills
till, later, later peasants in the valleys
felt in their bones disquieting kingdoms break

and matrons, by small cottages, would sense
implacable navies in their native wombs,
a generation of a harder wit

and later later when the senses quickened
(the hills being bare again) in a new season
in a night honoured with a desperate star

another head appeared, fiercer than these,
disdain flashed from his horns, a strange cry
perplexed the peasants, somnolent, appeased.

X

Deer on the high peaks, the wandering senses
are all, are all: fanatic heads deceive,
like branches springing in a true desert.

Smell now the cresses and the winter root,
passage of heather, journey of rank fox
mortal and moving on the strange hills.

In spring the raven and lascivious swallow,
migrant of air, the endless circle closing,
unclosing, closing, a bewildering ring

of natural marriage, pagan, sensuous.
Return of seasons, and the fugitive
Culloden of scents, erratic, hesitant.

The snow returning, and the summer wasp
more caustic than idea, hum of bees
at their devotions to the wild honey.

The hind crowned with her wanton sex,
rage of the sap in trees, the urgent salmon
pregnant with oceans dying into streams.

And these return in spite of the idea,
the direct reasoning road, the mad Ulysses
so unperverted, so implacable,

so wearing late his dull ironic crown
among a people he has never loved
nor felt in boredom kinship ominous

but fixed on a reasoned star his obstinate gaze
who came at last to where his childhood was
an infant island in an ancient place.

XI

Deer on the high peaks, let me turn
my gaze far from you, where the river winds
its slow way like an old man's argument.

The rocks obstinate, the rains persistent,
the stones ingathered into their chastened fury,
all things themselves, a fierce diversity.

The rampant egos of the flat plains,
the thorns gentle with their sour flowers,
tongues of the sharp stones, the water's business.

Contorted selves that twist in a dark wind,
far from the mountains, from the far and clear
ordered inventions of the stars ongoing.

And here, below, the water's business
smoothing the stone, consenting to the heads
that, easy of a summer, stare and stare

and speak:"I am, I am. Preserve me, O preserve.
Make me in mirror matchless and the earl
of such imagined kingdoms as endure.

I pray, I pray, a marchioness of this
dismembered kingdom, let my face be seen
not mortal now but of a lasting grace."

Roar of the waters, prickly thrust of thorn,
immutable stone, sand of a brute fact,
these are the maenads of necessity.

And the deer look down, Platonic dawn breaks
on Highland hills as distant as a thought,
an excellent Athens, obstinate mirage,

while the stone rears, the venomed stone rears
its savage being, and the waters pour
illusive summers to the real seas,

while the deer stand imperious, of a style,
make vibrant music, high and rich and clear,
mean what the plain mismeans, inform a chaos.

XII

Deer on the high hills, in your halfway kingdom,
uneasy in this, uneasy in the other,
but all at ease when earth and sky together

are mixed are mixed, become a royalty
none other knows, neither the migrant birds
nor the beasts chained to their instinctive courses.

That halfway kingdom is your royalty,
you on a meditative truth impaled,
the epicures of feeding absolutes,

you of a metaphysics still and proud,
native to air, native to earth both,
indigenous deer beneath a cloudburst sky;

to whom the lightning's native and the thunder,
whose sockets flash with an annunciant fire,
whose storms are vegetation's dearest friend.

Your antlers flash in light, your speed like thought
is inspiration decorous and assured,
a grace not theological but of

accomplished bodies, sensuous and swift,
of summer scents enjoyers, and of winters
the permanent spirits, watchful, unappeased:

of summer hills a speaking radiance
the body's language, excellent and pure,
discoursing love, free as the wandering wind:

of scentless winters the philosophers,
vigilant always like a tiptoe mind
on peaks of sorrow, brave and scrutinous:

on peaks of sorrow, brave and scrutinous,
on breakneck peaks, coherent and aplomb,
the image silent on the high hill.

XIII

Do colours cry? Does 'black' weep for the dead?
Is green so bridal, and is red the flag
and eloquent elegy of a martial sleep?

Are hills 'majestic' and devoted stones
plotting in inner distances our fall?
The mind a sea: and she a Helen who

in budding hours awakens to her new
enchanting empire all the summer day,
the keys of prisons dangling in her hands?

Is night a woman, and the moon a queen
or dowager of grace, and all the stars
archaic courtiers round ambiguous smiles?

Are rivers stories, and are plains their prose?
Are fountains poetry? And are rainbows the
wistful smiles upon a dying face?

And you, the deer, who walk upon the peaks,
are you a world away, a language distant?
Such symbols freeze upon my desolate lips!

XIV

There is no metaphor. The stone is stony.
The deer step out in isolated air.
We move at random on an innocent journey.

The rain is rainy and the sun is sunny.
The flower is flowery and the sea is salty.
My friend himself, himself my enemy.

The deer step out in isolated air.
Not nobles now but of a further journey.
Their flesh is distant as the air is airy.

The rivers torrents, and the grasses many.
The stars are starry, and the night nocturnal.
The fox a tenant of no other skin.

Who brings reports? There's one head to the penny.
A door is wooden, and no window grieves
for lovers turned away, for widows lonely.

The deer step out in isolated air.
The cloud is cloudy and the word is wordy.
Winter is wintry, lonely is your journey.

"You called sir did you?" "I who was so lonely
would speak with you: would speak to this tall chair,
would fill it chock-full of my melancholy."

So being lonely I would speak with any
stone or tree or river. Bear my journey,
you endless water, dance with a human joy.

This distance deadly! God or goddess throw me
a rope to landscape, let that hill, so bare,
blossom with grapes, the wine of Italy.

The deer step out in isolated air.
Forgive the distance, let the transient journey
on delicate ice not tragical appear

for stars are starry and the rain is rainy,
the stone is stony, and the sun is sunny,
the deer step out in isolated air.

Young Girl

Young girl who goes with a straight back on the street, there are baskets of flowers in my breast, my table is furnished with your laughter.

A woman will say to me, "There is pride in her walk." But I will answer as is fitting, "Is there pride in the sun in the sky? Is there jealousy between the stone and the gold?"

And when a storm goes past in its own world of rain and wind will you say, "Pride and arrogance" to it, as it turns forests upside down?

Will you speak disparagingly of the diamond because of its glitter or the sea because of its radiance? There is a white ship among the boats and among the black hats there is a crown.

You are at the Bottom of my Mind

Without my knowing it you are at the bottom of my mind, like one who visits the bottom of the sea with his helmet and his two great eyes: and I do not know properly your expression or your manner after five years of the showers of time pouring between you and me.

Nameless mountains of water pouring between me, hauling you on board, and your expression and manner in my weak hands. You went astray among the mysterious foliage of the sea-bottom in the green half-light without love.

And you will never rise to the surface of the sea, even though my hands should be ceaselessly hauling, and I do not know your way at all, you in the half-light of your sleep, haunting the bottom of the sea without ceasing, and I hauling and hauling on the surface of the ocean.

Going Home

Tomorrow I will go home to my island, trying to put a world into forgetfulness. I will lift a fistful of earth in my hands or I will sit on a hillock of the mind, watching "the shepherd with his sheep."

There will ascend (I presume) a thrush. A dawn or two will rise. A boat will be lying in the glitter of the western sun: and water will be running through the world of the similes of my intelligence.

But I will be thinking (in spite of that) of the great fire that is behind our thoughts, Nagasaki and Hiroshima, and I will hear in a room by myself a ghost or two constantly moving, the ghost of every error, the ghost of every guilt, the ghost of each time I walked past the wounded man on the stony road, the ghost of nothingness scrutinising my dumb room with distant face till the island is an ark rising and falling on a great sea and no one knowing whether the dove will ever return, and people talking and talking to each other, and the rainbow of forgiveness in their tears.

To an Old Woman

You are in the church listening, sitting on an uncomfortable bench to the words of one who is only half your age.

And I am sitting here writing these corrupted words, and not knowing whether it is the truth or the beautiful lie that is in my mind.

But there is one person who comes into my mind, you sitting in front of a pulpit in your simple black hat, and in your coat (black as well) and in your shoes that have walked many a long street with you.

You were not a scholar in your day. (Many a morning did you gut herring, and your hands were sore with salt, and the keen wind on the edge of your knife, and your fingers frozen with fire.)

You have never heard of Darwin or Freud or Marx or that other Jew, Einstein, with the brilliant mind: nor do you know the meaning of the dream you dreamed last night in your room in heavy sleep.

You haven't heard how the stars move away from us like calm queens through the sky. And you haven't heard how the lion with his fierce head sits at the table with us.

But you sit there in front of the pulpit and in your loneliness you say many a prayer and if the minister shakes you by the hand your mind is filled with happiness.

You remember other days, a sermon direct as a bullet, a summer pouring around a church, a gold ring and the testimony of roses opening summer like a new Bible in your memory.

And you will remember many a death and many days which went waste, a clock in the wall ticking your world to its end.

May your world prosper and you on your way home over the white streets like a man's mind, open with the edge of the knife, and boys standing in their quarrelsomeness studying nothingness: keenly they looked at you going without armour across a street burning at your feet, without armour but your harmonious spirit that never put a world in order but which will keep you, I hope, whole in your innocence like a coat.

The Old Woman

Tonight she is sitting by a window and the street like a bible below her eyes. The curtains have had many washings. There is a glitter from the flowered floor.

The world was once without shape, men and women like a red fever walking about flesh and mind, nostrils tasting love and anger.

Moon and sun in the sky, hand like salmon leaping to hand, the fish of the world in a net, pain that would not leave breast tranquil.

But everything has been set in order. Table in its place, chair in its place. This room is the mirror of her thoughts, arsenal from which will arise no music of growth.

For the music that will sing it together is youth itself that will never return. Her eye is sweeping the streets. Time is crouched in the window.

At the Cemetery

I saw them yesterday at the cemetery, with black hats, and the sun rising, a glitter of flowers about their feet, and one wearing a bitter shirt.

Glitter of the sky, a sea singing, a pouring of grass, and a steadiness of mountains, the mortal conversation of dark hats, the poetry of summer upside down.

A wide day extending to the horizon. A bible burning in the hands of the wind and sun, and a sea falling like an empty dress on that shore.

And he is where he is. My neighbour lying under the bee which murmurs among sweet flowers. It was death that killed him and not a bullet.

And a sun pouring, a sea pouring, black hats darkly sailing on a sea of roses, as there move poor words on a tide of music.

Eight Songs for a New Ceilidh

(1)

You asked me for a poem for yourself, thinking, I suppose, that I would put you among the stars for beauty and intelligence.

But as for me I grew up in bare Lewis without tree or branch and for that reason my mind is harder than the foolish babble of the heavens, and also at Hiroshima the kettle boiled over our music and in Belsen there was seen an example of dishonour eating love and flesh, and because of that and because of the truth and all the Evil that was done to us, and we ourselves did (among our complaints) I will never put a pen again into my fist for beauty or for intellect. Beauty is dangerous enough and as for the mind did it not spoil the glittering cities of Europe?

But when one night I shall hear the quarrelsome beasts of love I will make a song for you that will illuminate the murder of the deer in the heather.

(2)

When she took the great sea on her, Lewis went away and will not return. I was not compelled to sail 'over to Australia' but around me is Hiroshima and Pasternak's book is in my hands —

I will not drink a health-giving drink from the spring of the healthy deer of May but from water full of eels which are electric and shivering on my flesh like Venus breaking through the mind and the dark-green of the clouds but it was the fine bareness of Lewis that made the work of my mind like a loom full of the music of the miracles and greatness of our time.

(3)

I saw myself in a camp among the Nazis and the wretched Jews. My hand was white with the innocent lamps of Guernica and my cheek streaming with piteous tears but in one hand there was a hard gun while the gas was writhing like the mist of Lewis over cold rocks.

(4)

Standing at the end of the reservoir that was dumb, mena-cing, with bare water, I saw the live flies hitting the dead flies on the back. The foxglove was heavy about us with summer's perfume and the sky as limpid as the music of a fiddle. In that moment you leaped and went down, down into the water, and I was frightened that you wouldn't rise and I shouted in spite of the skill of my intelligence but after that I became silent.

(5)

I will not climb these mountains for what is at the top?

The stars are holding a ceilidh but what can they say that is not in my own dark depth? I will never sail on a ship. My Pacific is in my head and my Columbus praising countries that are far below. The day of my mind is my May and my twittering of birds the quick thoughts that are black and yellow about my skies.

(6)

I will never go to France, my dear, my dear, though you are young. I am tied to the Highlands. That is where I learnt my wound.

And are we not tied to that as well? A door will open but where will the slavish spirit of man go? I heard the wind blowing to the Greeks at the Pillars of Hercules: our round world is more harmonious than that. O, it is not a world of manliness that I am speaking of but about the guilt that follows me from mountain and moor. My Uist is inside my head and my love like an agonising tether that is yellow and dangerous and beautiful.

(7)

"Go to London," they said to me. "In the great city you will compose music from the bitter hard light of your stomach." And I was struggling with myself for many years, thinking of those streets, men with penetrating power in their faces, an illuminated glittering taxi flashing on the windows of my intelligence.

But tonight sitting at the fire and the hills between me and the sky and listening to the empty quietness and seeing the deer coming to my call I think of another one who said the truthful words: "Look straight down through wood and wood. Look in your own heart and write."

(8)

Will you go with me, young maiden, over to Japan where our sanity is wasting in that big bomb that fell on town and on mountain.

Not to Uist among the trees or to green Lewis among the heather nor a Farewell to Finnary burning calmly in the strait nor in the hall of Glasgow or Edinburgh and Duncan Ban walking elegantly with a bright gun among the lies that are clouds round our time.

When We Were Young

When we were young it would be raining and we throwing stones at the telegraph poles unceasingly.

One horse would be standing against a wall, drenched by the rain, his skin slippery with the grey rain.

When we were young we would be playing football, with the moon in the sky like a football made of gold.

When we were young old women would be telling us, "Don't do this, do that" for fear of the owl.

When we were young the sky would be empty, and pictures in the book, and the earth green and distant.

When we were young, there would be lies, when we are old the lie is that youth was without stain.

Freud

Great man from Vienna who opened the mind with a knife
keen with sore efficient happy light, and who saw the seas
sweating with the blue-green ghosts of plague, and un-
countable riches.

I follow the beasts with a joy I cannot tell though I should
be fishing from dungeon or from prison, as they move on
that sea-bottom in the freedom of truth with their great
helmets. No one will bring them to shore.

Cancer took your jaw away. But you were scanning with
profundity the bottom of that sea where there are horrifying
shadows. Father, mother and daughter fighting entwined
together in a Greek play, in a strangling of forests.

The letter that I will not send, the letter that I will not
keep, the poetry that my head cannot put together, the
history that I would not want anyone to tell of my planets,
the star is below in the seaweed of the skies.

Goodbye to the laughter of nature and the seas, goodbye
to the salt that will bring tears to thoughts, goodbye to
death which opens valuable countries, our rings are early
in the weddings of our gifts.

O miracle of the waves and I tirelessly scrutinising you
like a gay porpoise leaping in my country, it was you who
gave us these new waves — your monument is on the
bottom, and the seas are your pulpit.

The Prodigal Son

Under the stars of grief, the thin glass in his hand, like ice
which grows on pools, he listened to the dance. He listened
to that music, the melodeon of his loss, he listened to his
wounds in that golden distant country. His father running
like a bird on tiptoe of joy, his brother breaking up the
troublesome soil of dislike, the neighbours winking: "What

happened to you, dear? Wonderful the prosperity that has come on the little boy of our song."

What sort of place were you in? Is it beautiful, is it new? Is it wine that is in the well, whisky instead of water? Is there reaping without labour, is the autumn to your wish? Will corn be found in the barn on the great morning of the dew?

And the dance goes past, the dance of the planets and the people. He looked down inside the glass that was foolish and thin. He saw the stony eyes and he was filled with a sort of shivering and he sat there like a kettle on the dishonourable fire of the world.

And he heard the thunder of feet, the dance of past fashions. He felt again the rainstorms that spoilt the seasons before his step. He felt again the locks, the dangerous prison of lies. "O God, who put this spark in my breast in vain," he shouted in the unsteady winter and he threw the glass from his hand.

It turned over beneath the moon. It broke on the uncultivated soil. He got up and went home: "This place is as good as others," he shouted through the untellable music and the planets of a million laughters.

The Poppy

The flower of Flanders is red in the blue sky. That blood is still strong amidst the storm.

That red star is on my calm jacket. The hands are folded and the eyes are shut.

The potatoes are growing and the roots are so white, the dead bones among the water and the dew.

And the cows with their helmets and their great horns tasting grass that was cleansed by them and each skull quiet under the plough gently fertilising the earth far from heaven.

44

To My Mother

You were gutting herring in distant Yarmouth and the salt sun in the morning rising out of the sea, the blood on the edge of your knife, and that salt so coarse that it stopped you from speaking and made your lips bitter.

I was in Aberdeen sucking new courses, my Gaelic in a book and my Latin at the tiller, sitting there on a chair with my coffee beside me and leaves shaking the sails of scholarship and my intelligence.

Guilt is tormenting me because of what happened and how things are. I would not like to be getting up in the darkness of the day gutting and tearing the fish of the morning on the shore and that savage sea to be roaring down my gloves without cease.

Though I do that in my poetry it is my own blood that is on my hands, and every herring that the high tide gave me palpitating till I make a song, and instead of a cooper my language always hard and strict on me, and the coarse salt on my ring bringing animation to death.

I Build an Orange Church

I build an orange church and put inside it
a little orange minister in a pulpit
that's dandelion yellow.

I make a ceiling of intensest blue.
The seats are heliotrope, the bibles pink,
hymn books are apple green.

Picasso paints the walls with animals.
The angels swoop in red and there's a sun
of blinding nuclear light.

And so transform it all. . . . But for the guilt
that's small and black and creeps in when the door
swings on its oiled hinges.

What's Your Success?

What's your Success to me who read the great dead,
whose marble faces, consistent overhead,

outstare my verse? What are your chains to me,
your baubles and your rings? That scrutiny

turns on me always. Over terraced houses
these satellites rotate and in deep spaces

the hammered poetry of Dante turns
light as a wristwatch, bright as a thousand suns.

Hear Us O Lord

Hear us, O Lord, aggression is part of us.
You polish your jewellery in the salons of heaven.
Everything about you glitters, your wrist-watch, the diamond
at your invisible breast, below your invisible beard.

We are such ferocious animals, Lord, we're irrational.
The long journey of the lizard was propelled by this
to the green Jaguar standing in the driveway.
As you polish your nails we begin to hate you.

All those who tell us the truth we hate.
All those who were strong — like Hitler and Stalin — we loved.
We are obsessed by the table with the green light on it.
We practise with knives in the boudoir and the church.

Ah, if it were only a game. But all things happen.
Because we have spoken too much a heaven has fallen.
Because we have loved too much a door has been slammed.
We stare at the light of Envy green in the night.

What should we do to be saved? The screen slowly brightens.
You watch us with interest, a glass of pale wine in your hand.
"The things that they do, the plays that my actors perform."
We keep you alive in the silence, in an absence of angels.

At the Highland Games

Like re-reading a book which has lost its pith.

Watching the piper dandying over a sodden stage
saluting an empty tent.

The empty beer glasses catch the sun
sparkle like old brooches against green.

Fur-hatted, with his huge twirling silver stick
the pipe-major has gypsy cheekbones, colour of brick.

Everything drowses. The stewards with aloof eagle stare
sit on collapsing rock, chair on brown chair.

Once the pibroch showed the grave 'ground'
of seas without bubbles, where great hulks were drowned,

meat with moustaches. The heroic dead die
over and over the sea to misty Skye.

Past the phantom ivy, bird song, I walk
among crew-cuts, cameras, the heather-covered rock,

past my ancestry, peasants, men who bowed
with stony necks to the daughter-stealing lord.

Past my ancestry, the old songs, the pibroch
stirring my consciousness like the breeze a loch.

Past my buried heart my friend who complains
of "All the crime, their insane violence."

Stone by stone the castles crumble. The seas
have stored away their great elegies.

"Morag of Dunvegan." Dandy piper
with delicate soft paws, knee-bending stepper,

saluting an empty tent. Blue-kilted stewards
strut like strange storks along the sodden sward.

Finished. All of it's finished. The Gaelic
boils in my mouth, the South Sea silver stick

twirls, settles. The mannequins are here.
Calum, how you'd talk of their glassy stare,

their loud public voices. Stained pictures
of what was raw, violent, alive and coarse.

I watch their heirs, Caligulas with canes
stalk in their rainbow kilts towards the dance.

In the Classics Room

In summer how lovely the girls are
even here where Vergil is king of the walk,

where the hooded owl eyes have brooded all winter
on a text, a lacuna, a gap in a line
where the power is undischarged

and the dusty bulbs swung metrically in a draught
blowing in from the Western Sea.

How easy it was to forget them, the girls,
how easy to believe they were only dresses,
satchels, hollow heads to be filled with poetry.

Now it is they themselves who fill with poetry
brimming each day with more and more of their wine.

O Dido, in your pillar of fire
excessively burning in Carthage,
who is this Aeneas whose wood has grown subtle

who is this Roman whose glasses reflect your fire
whose legs twitch uncontrollably like an infant's
whose book shakes like a leaf?

The Departing Island

Strange to see it — how as we lean over
this vague rail, the island goes away
into its loved light grown suddenly foreign:
how the ship slides outward, like a cold ray
from a sun turned cloudy, and rough land draws down
into an abstract sea its arranged star.

Strange how it's like a dream when two waves past,
and the engine's hum puts villages out of mind
or shakes them together in a waving fashion.
The lights stream northward down a wolfish wind.
A pacing passenger wears the air of one
whom tender arms and fleshly hands embraced.

It's the island that goes away, not we who leave it.
Like an unbearable thought it sinks beyond
assiduous reasoning light and wringing hands,
or, as a flower roots deep into the ground,
it works its darkness into the gay winds
that blow about us in a later spirit.

To Have Found One's Country

To have found one's country
after a long journey
and it to be here
around one all the time.
It is like taking a girl
from the house next door,
after all that travel
that black dense wall.

To have fallen in love with
stone, thistle and strath,
to see the blood flow
in wandering old rivers,
this wound is not stanched
by handkerchiefs or verse.
This wound was after all
love and a deep curse.

Now I'm frightened to name it
lest some witch should spring
screaming out of the tombs
with a perverted broom.
I'm almost frightened to
name all the waters,
these seas, tall hills,
these misty bordered bibles.

Love's such a transient thing
except for that hard slogging
which, though it's love, we don't
name it by that ring
in which, tortured, we fight
with all the bones about us
in these cemeteries that hold
the feet in living grass.

Jean Brodie's Children

Jean Brodie's children in your small green caps,
I hear you twitter down the avenues.

The great round bells ring out, the Mademoiselle
despairs of English. In the rustling dorms
you giggle under sheets.

"Dear Edinburgh, how I remember you,
your winter cakes and tea, your bright red fire,
your swirling cloaks and clouds.

Your grammar and your Greek, the hush of leaves,
No Orchids for Miss Blandish with a torch
beneath the tweedy blanket.

Ah, those beautiful days, all green and shady,
our black and pleated skirts, our woollen stockings,
our ties of a calm mauve.

Mistresses, iron in their certainty,
their language unambiguous, but their lives
trembling on grey boughs."

She Teaches Lear

Much to have given up? Martyr, one says?
And to read *Lear* to these condemning ones
in their striped scarves and ties but in the heart
tall, cool and definite. Naval, in this art.
"Brought it on himself. He ran away,
then strained to keep his pomp and circumstance."

Of course it's true. Much to be said for Regan,
Goneril too. Cordelia just a tune,
and also beautiful as I am not.
"Life must be lived. Life is beyond thought.
These two were living." Who says that? It's Brown.
The smallest one (with glasses) in the room.

So I go home towards his bitterness,
achieved selfishness, clinging so with claws
to chair and pipe, a dreadful bitter man.
He hates all life, yet lives. Helpless in pain,
trains pain on others. "Pray," at night he says,
"undo this button," and yet hates for this

me out of helplessness. And yet I stay.
"Regan and Goneril had some place to go."
("Some*where*." Correct this young American.)
Which side is right? For there is young pale Jean —
she might be one. Responsibility
is weighty, living, in the to-and-fro

of these cool deadly judgements. So she listens,
the true Cordelia, library-white face,
thin-boned and spectacled, speechlessly unhappy,
and ready for all art, especially poetry.
"They had some place to go and pure passions.
The rest's hypocrisy." Purity of the race?

No, not as far as that. Simply a lie,
to live and feed with one so selfish grown
as age is always selfish. The proud two
spur their tall horses into the bright blue
in search of lust, are willing so to die,
the absolute hunters, Goneril and Regan,

beautiful too with their own spare beauty
when one forgets the haunted piteous fox
(there's always a fox whenever such ride by).
Does Jean, as I do, sniff it? Memory
of dear addictive fences, of the high
tall splendid brutes, past little dreaming flocks.

And yet . . . More simply. They are what they are,
I am what I am? The sensitive eye
broods by packed windows of interior pain
fastened to writhings, knowing rages mean
often unhappiness, that old men wear
their stubborn angers out of dignity,

the failing vigour — eyes, arms, knees.
Gravity pulls them down into the ground.
Last anger blossoms on its final lip.
"Lear is a child," I hear. Is this the deep
Greek brilliant irony? I find my peace
in this dictator because I have no kind

child to nourish. No, it's not quite that.
"We'll come to this," I cry. "No," Moira says,
quite definite and calm. "If I should come
to such a state let all drive me from home."
Easy enough, I think (but hold the thought)
to speak such words when interested praise

makes your face happy at the Saturday
school-club dance, in yellow, and a hand
glides down your bare arm, it seems, forever.
Why should I speak, this loud, my own fever?
And then I know it's right as far's mind may
(without sly falsity) seek to understand.

"It's just in case," I say, "in case, malformed"—
(how vulnerable ties and scarves, how pure!)
"by living we are made. It's just in case"—
the need, the need! — Polite and curious
they know of no such need (but Jean). Not armed
nor yet disarmed they sit. Sure or unsure

it hasn't touched them yet, the fear of age.
Regan and Goneril seem more natural.
From our own weakness only are we kind.
Admire such ones but know in your own mind
how they would bring upon us innocent carnage,
the end of Lear, and *Lear*, their own worse will.

At the Sale

Old beds, old chairs, old mattresses, old books.
Old pictures of coiffed women, hatted men,
ministers with clamped lips and flowing beards,
a Duke in his Highland den,
and, scattered among these, old copper fire-guards,
stone water-bottles, stoves and shepherds' crooks.

How much goes out of fashion and how soon!
The double-columned leather-covered tomes
recall those praying Covenanters still
adamant against Rome's
adamant empire. Every article
is soaked in time and dust and sweat and rust. What tune

warbled from that phonograph? Who played
that gap-toothed dumb piano? Who once moved
with that white chamber pot through an ancient room?
And who was it that loved
to see her own reflection in the gloom
of that webbed mirror? And who was it that prayed

holding that Bible in her fading hands?
The auctioneer's quick eyes swoop on a glance,
a half-seen movement. In the inner ring
a boy in serious stance
holds up a fan, a piece of curtaining,
an hour-glass with its trickle of old sand.

We walk around and find an old machine.
On one side pump, on another turn a wheel.
But nothing happens. What's this object for?
Imagine how we will
endlessly pump and turn for forty years
and then receive a pension, smart and clean,

climbing a dais to such loud applause
as shakes the hall for toiling without fail
at this strange nameless gadget, pumping, turning,
each day oiling the wheel
with zeal and eagerness and freshness burning
in a happy country of anonymous laws,

while the ghostly hands are clapping and the chairs
grow older as we look, the pictures fade,
the stone is changed to rubber, and the wheel
elaborates its rayed
brilliance and complexity and we feel
the spade become a scoop, cropping the grass,

and the flesh itself becomes unnecessary.
O hold me, love, in this appalling place.
Let your hand stay me by this mattress here
and this tall ruined glass,
by this dismembered radio, this queer
machine that waits and has no history.

Old Woman with Flowers

These are your flowers. They were given to you
so nurse them carefully and tenderly.
Though flowers grow freely elsewhere, here in this room
there's not much space, so therefore like a child
let no one else go near them.
                              O dear God
wherever you are, I am almost driven wild
by your frightening flowers whose blossoms are turned to bone
for an old woman to look at, in a small room alone.

Old Woman

Overwhelmed with kindnesses — and you have nothing.
They bring you roses to refresh their hearts
and still the bitter voices.

They greet you sweetly, you are now their child,
they flatter you completely,
and you have nothing to present to them
objects to objects, just your used self.

Only a god I think could take such gifts
and not feel hatred. Only a god could bear
such manifold penances, and be the vase
for all these guilty roses.

You are no god and therefore should you snap
suddenly out at them between old teeth
like a fox dying in a sweet country
I should not turn from that poor twisted face
bayed in its autumn by solicitous smiles.

If You are about to Die Now

If you are about to die now
there is nothing I can write for you.
History is silent about this.
Even Napoleon, face huge as a plate,
disguised the advance guard and said:
"Why they sent for my brother is because
he, and not I, is in trouble."

The screens come down. The nurses disappear
like the tails of fishes. The clouds
are white as cotton wool and also
Dettol outlives the perfume.
The unshaven man in the next ward
is given Shaving Lotion for Christmas.
Sorrow stands like a stork on one leg,
brooding.

The coloured windows give way to plain.
The horsemen crossing the moor are comrades
going the other way into the country
of the undisciplined and the free.

Here there is the Land of the Straight Lines
with a banner black and silent,
a black mirror
with the image of an old rose.

History does not warn us of this.
Napoleon's face expands to a window.
The manic thoughts fly outwards, beating.
"The documents did not tell me.
There was no announcement in the salon.
Why is it that the chairs are getting crooked?
Why is it that my army does not hear me?
They are eating, laughing by the stream.

I shout to them, 'Put on your armour.'
But they do not listen.
They do not know me, they are relapsing
into the marsh of their idleness.
They are schoolboys escaped from Latin.
O how afraid they are of Excellence.
They admire their faces in the water.

They splash in the new bubbles."

from *The White Air of March*

(1)

This is the land God gave to Andy Stewart —
    we have our inheritance.
There shall be no ardour, there shall be indifference.
There shall not be excellence, there shall be the average.
We shall be the intrepid hunters of golf balls.

Have you not known, have you not heard, has it not been reported
that Mrs Macdonald has given an hour-long lecture on Islay
and at the conclusion was presented with a bouquet of flowers
by Marjory, aged five?
                              Have you not noted
the photograph of the whist drive, skeleton hands,
rings on skeleton fingers?
                              Have you not seen
the glossy weddings in the glossy pages,
champagne and a 'shared joke.'
                              Do you not see
the Music Hall's still alive here in the North? and on the stage
the yellow gorse is growing.
                              "Tragedy," said Walpole, "for those
                                            who feel.
For those who think, it's comic."
                              Pity then those who feel
and, as for the Scottish Soldier, off to the wars!
The Cuillins stand and will forever stand.
Their streams scream in the moonlight.

(2)

The Cuillins tower
clear and white.
In the crevices the Gaelic bluebells flower.

(Eastward
Culloden
where the sun shone
on the feeding raven.
Let it be forgotten!)

The Cuillins tower
scale on scale.
The music of the imagination must be restored,
upward.

(The little Highland dancer
in white shirt green kilt
regards her toe
arms akimbo.
Avoids the swords.)

To avoid the sword
is death.
            To walk the ward
of Dettol, loss of will,
where old men watch the wall,
eyes in a black wheel,
and the nurse in a starched dress
changes the air.

The Cuillins tower
tall and white.
March breeds white sails.

The eagle soars.
On the highest peaks
The sharpest axe.

(8)

The exiles have departed,
                    leaving old houses.
The Wind wanders like an old man who has lost his mind.
"What do you want?" asks the wind. "Why are you crying?
Are those your tears or the rain?"
I do not know. I touch my cheek. It is wet.
I think it must be the rain.

It is bitter
to be an exile in one's own land.
It is bitter
to walk among strangers
    when the strangers are in one's own land.

It is bitter
to dip a pen in continuous water
to write poems of exile
in a verse without honour or style.

(9)

There have been so many
exiles.
      Jews
turn on their limited space
like cows.
      So many
faces blank as watches
telling
      nothing but time.

How can you drink a cup of wine
without tasting the vinegar
without feeling the thorn?

On the high far
Cuillins
I see them climb.

(12)

The tall buses pass by.
      The cottages trail their roses.

Look at the witch at the waterfall.
      She does Bed and Breakfast.

"Ah, Freedom is a noble thing."

      Around the Cuillins
the clouds drift like green dollars.

The Cuillins tower high in the air —
                              Excellence.
We climb from pain to perfume:
the body opens out; gullies,
crevices, reveal the orchis.
The soul flies skyward,
impregnated with scent.
On the right hand
        the sun will tenant
Skye.
            The mist dissipates.
Gold grows at our feet.

(16)

            Excellence!
"costing not less than everything"
Illusion after illusion dies.
After the gay green, the blackness.
Snatches
"and I mysel in crammasie."
Rainbows
out of the darkness.
Green,
green moments
or out of the waterfall
a sudden face —
so dearly known and killed.
Minotaur of guilt
coiled at the centre, vivid.
Flashes.
Blades.
Rotors of Glasgow knives.
Irises
held over tenements
intent, inventing,
Periphrases,

white deer stepping by Loch Lomond side.
The dead bury their dead.
The machines finished
underground.

In the white air of March
a new mind.

The TV

(1)

The sun rises every day
from moving shadows —
on the TV.

(2)

We did not believe in the existence of Ireland
till we saw it many nights —
on the TV.

(3)

He knows more about Humphrey Bogart
than he knows about Big Norman —
since he got the TV.

(4)

Said Plato —
"We are tied in a cave"—
that is, the TV.

(5)

A girl came into the room
without perfume without expression —
on the TV.

63

(6)

At last he lost the world
As Berkeley said —
there was nothing but the TV.

(7)

He bought 'War and Peace,'
I mean Tolstoy,
after seeing it on the TV.

(8)

When he switched off the TV
the world went out —
he himself went out.

(9)

His hands did not come back to him
or his eyes
till he put on the TV.

(10)

A rose in a bowl on the TV set,
the things that are in the world,
the things that are not.

(11)

He found himself in the story.
He was in the room.
He didn't know where he was.

(12)

You, my love, are dearer to me
than Softly Softly
than Sportsnight with Coleman.

"In locked rooms with iron gates"—
but, my love,
do they have TV?

Shall Gaelic Die?

(Translated by the author)

(1)

A picture has no grammar. It haś neither evil nor good. It has only colour, say orange or mauve.
Can Picasso change a minister? Did he make a sermon to a bull?
Did heaven rise from his brush? Who saw a church that is orange?
In a world like a picture, a world without language, would your mind go astray, lost among objects?

(2)

Advertisements in neon, lighting and going out, "Shall it . . . shall it . . . Shall Gaelic . . . shall it . . . shall Gaelic . . . die?"

(3)

Words rise out of the country. They are around us. In every month in the year we are surrounded by words.
Spring has its own dictionary, its leaves are turning in the sharp wind of March, which opens the shops.
Autumn has its own dictionary, the brown words lying on the bottom of the loch, asleep for a season.
Winter has its own dictionary, the words are a blizzard building a tower of Babel. Its grammar is like snow.
Between the words the wild-cat looks sharply across a No-Man's-Land, artillery of the Imagination.

4

They built a house with stones. They put windows in the house, and doors. They filled the room with furniture and the beards of thistles.

They looked out of the house on a Highland world, the flowers, the glens, distant Glasgow on fire.

They built a barometer of history.

Inch after inch, they suffered the stings of suffering.

Strangers entered the house, and they left.

But now, who is looking out with an altered gaze? What does he see?

What has he got in his hands? A string of words.

5

He who loses his language loses his world. The Highlander who loses his language loses his world.

The space ship that goes astray among planets loses the world.

In an orange world how would you know orange? In a world without evil how would you know good?

Wittgenstein is in the middle of his world. He is like a spider.

The flies come to him. 'Cuan' and 'coill' rising.*

When Wittgenstein dies, his world dies.

The thistle bends to the earth. The earth is tired of it.

I came with a 'sobhrach' in my mouth. He came with a 'primrose.'

A 'primrose by the river's brim.' Between the two languages, the word 'sobhrach' turned to 'primrose'.

Behind the two words, a Roman said 'prima rosa.'

The 'sobhrach' or the 'primrose' was in our hands. Its reasons belonged to us.

* 'Cuan' means 'sea' and 'coill' means 'wood.'

"That thing about which you cannot speak, be silent about it." Was there a pianist before a piano? Did Plato have a melodeon? Melodeon in the heavens? Feet dancing in the heavens? Red lips and black hair? Was there a melodeon in the heavens? A skeleton of notes.

"Shall Gaelic die?" A hundred years from now who will say these words? Who will say, "Co their?"* Who? The voice of the owl.

If I say 'an orange church' will I build an orange church?
If I say 'a mauve minister' will I create him?
The tartan is in its own country.
The tartan is a language.
A Campbell is different from a Macdonald (this is what a tartan teaches).
The tartans fight each other. Is that why they had to put a colourless church between them?

Said Alexander Macdonald, "It was Gaelic that Adam and Eve spoke in that garden." Did God speak Gaelic as well, when he told them about the apple? And when they left that garden, were they like exiles sailing to . . . Canada?

Shall Gaelic die! What that means is: shall we die?

An orange church with green walls. A picture on a wall showing ships like triangles. On another wall, a picture of a cafe with men made of paint. 'Gloria Deo' in the language

---

* 'Co their?' — 'Who will say?'

of paintings, an orange bell, a yellow halo around the pulpit
where there are red dancers.

(13)

Were you ever in a maze? Its language fits your language.
Its roads fit the roads of your head. If you cannot get out of
the language you cannot get out of the maze. Its roads
reflect your language. O for a higher language, like a hawk
in the sky, that can see the roads, that can see their end, like
God who built the roads, our General Wade. The roads of
the Highlands fit the roads of our language.

(14)

When the ape descended from the trees he changed his
language. He put away the green leaves. He made small
sharp words, words which made stones.

(15)

The dove returned to Noah with a word in his mouth.

(16)

The scholar is sitting with a candle in front of him. He is
construing words. He is building a dictionary. Little by
little, inch by inch, he is building a dictionary. Outside the
window the children are shouting, a ball is rising to the
sky, a girl and a boy are walking without language to bed.
What will he do when the ball enters the quiet room,
stopping him at B, and Z so distant.

(17)

Whom have you got in the net? Who is rising with green
eyes, with a helmet, who is in the net?
Cuchulain is in the net, he is rising from the sea, ropes of
moonlight at his heels, ropes of language.

(18)

"When you turn your back on the door, does the door
exist?" said Berkeley, the Irishman who was alive in the
soul.
When the Highlands loses its language, will there be a
Highlands, said I, with my two coats, losing, perhaps, the
two.

(19)

A million colours are better than one colour, if they are
different.
A million men are better than one man if they are different.
Keep out of the factory, O man, you are not a robot. It
wasn't a factory that made your language — it made you.

(20)

Like a rainbow, like crayons, spectrum of beautiful lan-
guages. The one-language descended like a church — like a
blanket, like mist.

(21)

God is outside language, standing on a perch. He crows
now and again. Who hears him? If there is a God let him
emanate from the language, a perfume emanating from the
dew of the morning, from the various-coloured flowers.

(22)

Death is outside the language. The end of language is
beyond language. Wittgenstein didn't speak after his death.
What language would he speak? In what language would
you say, 'Fhuair a' Ghaidhlig bas?'*

(23)

When the name 'Adam' was called, he turned his back on
the hills. He saw his shadow at his feet — he drew his
breath.

* 'Fhuair a' Ghaidhlig bas' — 'Gaelic is dead.'

You cannot say, 'Not-Adam.' You cannot say 'Not-Eve.'
The apple has a name as well. It is in the story.

The gold is new. It will not rust. 'Immutable universal,' as
the Frenchman said. But the pennies, the pounds, the half-
crowns, these coins that are old and dirty, the notes that are
wrinkled like old faces, they are coping with time; to these I
give my allegiance, to these I owe honour, the sweetness.
'Immutable, perfect,' Midas with his coat of gold and of
death.

For John Maclean, Headmaster, and Classical and Gaelic Scholar

(1)

The coloured roses fade along the wall.
How shall we live? How perfectly they fall,
the October leaves in yellow, how exact
the woods appear, so married to the fact
of their own unwilled and accurate funeral
without interrogation. In this tract

the dazzling hearse has led us to, we stand,
hats in our hands. The serious piper plays
'The Lament for the Children' and we hear the bound
and ribboned bouquets thudding. Then we take our ways
to the waiting cars across unechoing ground

or over crackling gravel. It remains,
the body in the casket, and begins
its simple mineral weathering. We return
to our complex human burning. What we mourn
changes as we mourn it, and routines
wed and enring us as we move and burn.

(2)

For you it was the case that Homer lived
in our fluorescence, that Ulysses homed
through our stained and plaguey light, that Hector grieved
in his puncturable armour, that engraved
even in Skye was marble which consumed
the bodies of live Greeks who shaped and carved

contemporary sculpture. Under leaves
which dappled your warm garden (as the groves
of autumnal classic Greece) you turned a page
or made an emendation in a passage.
Exactitude's a virtue, so believes
the inveterate scholar. Happy who can judge

evil as a hiatus or a false
quantity in harmony, who knows
that what protects us from the animals
is language healthy as a healthy pulse
and that our moral being can like prose
be manifestly tested where it fails.

(3)

I know that it is waning, that clear light
that shone on all our books and made them white
with unanswerable grammar. That the slaves
sustained our libraries and that the wolves
and watchful eagles nourished an elite
and that the elegant and forceful proofs

71

of their geometers will not suffice.
I know that Athene is wandering now,
dishevelled in the shrubbery, and the nurse
beckons at evening to her. Gods rehearse
their ruined postures and the ruined brow
reflects from mirrors not of fire but ice

and that our brute Achilles drives his wheels
across the gesturing shadows: and that kneels
to cheering legions Aphrodite: packs
are watching Ajax hacking with his axe
inanely the pale sheep: and shady deals
illuminate Odysseus's tracks.

(4)

You were a teacher also: what we've learned
is also what we teach: and what we are
cannot be hidden, though we walk black-gowned
along the radiant corridors, profound
in serious scholarship and that precious star
proposed by art or conscience. Where you burned

exactitude prevailed, the rule of Rome,
the gravitas of Brutus and his calm,
his stoic tenderness, his love of books,
his principles and practice. For the Dux
stands in his place, the overwhelming psalm
enchants him wholly among clean-limbed Greeks,

and if you touch him he gives out true coin.
Echo on echo, pupils make a world
which is their bronze and yours, and they will join
link on bright link to make the legions shine
with ethics and with elegance. The absurd
becomes a simple weather, clear and fine.

(5)

The October leaves are falling. None condemns
their seasonal abdication. What consumes
their crowns and robes is natural, a law
that's common to the weasel and the crow.
They hear no music of the funeral drums
and no corteges shade the way they go

no mountains brood, nor does the sharp wind mourn
nor tragic clouds move slowly. For the ice
steadily thickens over lake and corn.
In this pure azure there's no paradise
nor the hell nor purgatory that we devise
lest in the world we shiver and we burn

without the falcon's unhistorical aim,
its brutal beak, the momentary tomb
of its spontaneous moments. Or the sheep
that grazes in its own forgetful sleep
or the barbarians that struck at Rome,
its pompous destiny and shadowed hope.

(6)

Though it is finished now, that scholarship,
though vases crack and hourly we may graze
on superficial quanta: though we sleep
abandoned to disorder, and the days
are flashes of small light: and what we praise
is transient and odd, we yet may keep

pictures of autumn, graver, more restrained,
with a finer balance of the weighty mind,
a wind from Rome and Greece which held our course
steady to a harbour where salt oars
received their justice and to scales assigned
the soul would shiver with a stronger force

which now in neon vibrates. But in light
(let it be legend) accompanied the leaves
to their natural assignations and the fruit
bowed to a holy earth. The swan that moves
in reedy waters bows its neck. The waves
receive it, flesh and shadow, day and night.

(7)

So with your battered helmet let you be
immersed in golden autumn as each tree
accepts its destiny and will put by
its outworn crown, its varying finery,
and let the humming of the latest bee
bear its last honey home. Beneath this sky

the hexagonal coffin crowned with flowers restores
your body to the earth from which we came
to build our shaking ladders. What was yours
was no phantasmal order, and your name
planted in this place held to its aim
from wider deeper origins. If there were pyres

then a pyre you should have had, and lictors too.
And phantom legions. In this perfect blue
imagine therefore flame that's amber, yellow,
leaves of good flame, volumes that burn and glow,
the foliage of your autumn, where you grew
and where you are buried in the earth you know.

On a Summer's Day

Thus it is.
There is much loneliness
and the cigarette coupons will not save us.

I have studied your face across the draughtsboard.
It is freckled and young.
Death and summer have such fine breasts.

Tanned, they return from the sea.
The colour of sand, their blouses the colour of waves,
they walk in the large screen of my window.

Bacon, whose Pope screams in the regalia
of chairs and glass, dwarf of all the ages,
an hour-glass of ancient Latin,

you have fixed us where we are, cacti able to talk,
twitched by unintelligible tornadoes,
snakes of collapsing sand.

They trail home from the seaside in their loose blouses.
The idiot bounces his ball as they pass.
He tests his senile smile.

Dead for a Rat

What snarls
in the corner?
It wants to live
It bares its teeth at you.

It wants to live
more than you do
Its whole body
trembles
with its want to live.

The fur arches from its body
Its green eyes spark
Its lips are drawn back from the teeth
It hates you.

It hates you
more than you hate it.
Hamlet
lie down
in the sound of the trumpet

It quests you Hamlet
Will you go
behind the arras
behind the tapestry
will you go
Hamlet
with all the weight
of your bright thought
upon you?

Will you go Hamlet
in your shuttling armour
in your whirr
of literature
with your French rapier
sparkling, veering?

How Often I Feel like You

Ah, you Russians, how often I feel like you
full of ennui, hearing the cry of wolves
on frontiers of green glass.
In the evening
one dreams of white birches and of bears.
There are picnics in bright glades and someone talking

endlessly of verse as if mowing grass,
endlessly of philosophy round and round
like a red fair with figures of red soldiers
spinning forever at their 'Present Arms.'
How long it takes for a letter to arrive.
Postmen slog heavily over the steppes
and drop their dynamite through the letter-box.
For something is happening everywhere but here.
Here there are Hamlets and old generals.
Everyone sighs and says 'Ekh' and in the stream
a girl is swimming naked among gnats.
This space is far too much for us like time.
Even the clocks have asthma. There is honey,
herring and jam and an old samovar.
Help us, let something happen, even death.
God has forgotten us. We are like fishers
with leather leggings dreaming in a stream.

End of Schooldays

Captains, this is your last day in school.
You won't wear these helmets any more.
Do you not hear the whisper in the triumph,
like a suspect heart? Do you not see
how Mr Scott, though kind, is harried
by voices inaudibly calling from his house.

Look out on the fields. Never again will you see
such a sweet greenness, as of colours leaving
a place where they've been happy for a while.
The harness is turning now to other horses.
Laughter comes up the road and mounts the brae.
The names on the doors are rewriting themselves.

Never mind, the music will not leave you
or not completely. Sometimes in a betrayal,
in the middle of a deal just turning rancid,
after the fifth gin, the fifth fat hand,
the cloudy globes, set on the cloth, you'll hear it,

the music of your Ideal, quietly humming
in locker-rooms that smell of sweat and rain.
You'll be coming home in a warm and eerie light,
legs tall and willowy, in your hand the cup,
shaking a little, in your flabby hand
the trembling cup, in your old grasping hand.

For Keats

Genius is so strange,
you were in so many ways ordinary
in so many ways wounded like us.

But the vase beckons —
continually the vase beckons —
the imperfect bird sings
in the brown mortal leaves.

Poor Tom dies in the white linen.
Sore throats! Do nightingales have sore throats?
In the nightingale's pure notes
what eloquent disease?

Happily to seek the classic —
that land without fatigue —
that which stands like the rocks of Staffa
black remarkable architecture of the sea
solider than weeping Skye.

Than the grass of summer,
devotees of England's spas,
the irritabilities of the second rate,
the helmet bruised and vain.

Fighting the scree, to arrive at Autumn,
innocent impersonal accepted
where the trees do not weep like gods
but are at last themselves.

Bristly autumn, posthumous and still,
the crowning fine frost on the hill
the perfect picture blue and open-eyed
with the lakes as fixed as your brother's eyes,
autumn that will return

and will return and will return, however
the different delicate vase revolves
in the brown mortal foliage, in the woods
of egos white as flowers.

Gaelic Songs

I listen to these songs
from a city studio.
They belong to a different country,
to a barer sky,
to a district of heather and stone.
They belong to the sailors
who kept their course
through nostalgia and moonlight.
They belong to the maidens
who carried the milk in pails
home in the twilight.
They belong to the barking of dogs,

to the midnight of stars,
to the sea's terrible force,
exile past the equator.
They belong to the sparse grass,
to the wrinkled faces,
to the houses sunk in the valleys,
to the mirrors
brought home from the fishing.

Now they are made of crystal
taking just a moment
between two programmes
elbowing them fiercely
between two darknesses.

In the Chinese Restaurant

Because we'd never go there, it was good,
those years together. We'd never need to go
though we could talk of it and so we were
happy together in a place we'd made
so small and airless that we couldn't leave.
But we could think of it and say, "Perhaps
we'll go there someday." But we could not go
for as we lived so we'd lost all the maps.
It grew more perfect as the slow years passed
as if we were there already. One fine day
we'd find it all around us if we looked.
We would be in it, even old and grey.

So that, one night, in that late restaurant
with Chinese waiters round us we picked up
the menu in Chinese and understood
every single word of it. It was
a revelation when the waiters smiled.
They looked so clear as the glasses slowly filled.

Christmas 1971

There's no snow this Christmas . . . there was snow
when we received the small horses and small cart,
brothers together all those years ago.
There were small watches made of liquorice
surrealist as time hung over chairs.
I think perhaps that when we left the door
of the white cottage with its fraudulent icing
we were quite fixed as to our different ways.
Someone is waving with black liquorice hands
at the squashed windows as the soundless bells
and the soundless whips lash our dwarf horses forward.
We diverge at the road-end in the whirling snow
never to meet but singing, pulling gloves
over and over our disappearing hands.

In the Time of the Useless Pity

In the time of the useless pity I turned away
from your luminous clock-face in the hopeless dark,
appealing to me greenly, appealing whitely.
Nothing I could do, I had tried everything,
lain flat on the rug, fluttered my spaniel paws,
offered you my house like an unlocked crystal —
and so it came, the time of the useless pity
when the roots had had enough of you, when they slept,
elaborating themselves by themselves
when they shifted over from yours, seeking a place
different from yours to burst through and to pierce
with a royal purple, straight and delicate: sails
of the suave petals unfurling at the mast.

Finis not Tragedy

All is just. The mouth you feed turns on you
if not truly fed, the machine clicks
accurately in a new house.

The will that you abolished stands slackly
when you need it most, the vanquished
muscles will not answer.

The machine, powered by history, clicks
shut like a filing cabinet and on it
you read Finis not Tragedy.

Nothing is there that wasn't there.
No memos that you haven't read
over and over again

when your skull-faced secretary stood smiling
as you tore papers into little pieces
and hummed through your clenched teeth

and turning you said to him "Remember honour.
Tell the story as it really was."
But he is silent, smiling.

Everything is Silent

Everything is silent now
before the storm.
The transparent walls tremble.
You can hear the very slightest hum
of a stream miles away.

The silence educates your ear.
The threat is palpable.
You can hear the boots beyond the mountains.
You can hear the breathings of feathers.
You can hear the well of your heart.

You know what it is that permits the walls,
that allows the ceiling,
that lets the skin cling to your body,
that mounts the spiral
of your beholden bones.

That sorrow is a great sorrow
and leaves you radiant
when the tempest has passed
and your vases are still standing
and your bones are stalks in the water.

You Lived in Glasgow

You lived in Glasgow many years ago.
I do not find your breath in the air.
It was, I think, in the long-skirted thirties
when idle men stood at every corner
chewing their fag-ends of a failed culture.
Now I sit here in George Square
when the War Memorial's yellow sword glows bright
and the white stone lions mouth at bus and car.
A maxi-skirted girl strolls slowly by.
I turn and look. It might be you. But no.
Around me there's a 1970 sky.

Everywhere there are statues. Stone remains.
The mottled flesh is transient. On those trams,
invisible now but to the mind, you bore
your groceries home to the 1930 slums.

"There was such warmth," you said. The gaslight hums
and large caped shadows tremble on the stair.
Now everything is brighter. Pale ghosts walk
among the spindly chairs, the birchen trees.
In lights of fiercer voltage you are less
visible than when in winter you
walked, a black figure, through the gaslight blue.

The past's an experience that we cannot share.
Flat-capped Glaswegians and the Music Hall.
Apples and oranges on an open stall.
A day in the country. And the sparkling Clyde
splashing its local sewage at the wall.
This April day shakes memories in a shade
opening and shutting like a parasol.
There is no site for the unshifting dead.
You're buried elsewhere though your flickering soul
is a constant tenant of my tenement.

You were happier here than anywhere, you said.
Such fine good neighbours helping when your child
almost died of croup. Those pleasant Wildes
removed with the fallen rubble have now gone
in the building programme which renews each stone.
I stand in a cleaner city, better fed,
in my diced coat, brown hat, my paler hands
leafing a copy of the latest book.
Dear ghosts, I love you, haunting sunlit winds,
dear happy dented ghosts, dear prodigal folk.

I left you, Glasgow, at the age of two
and so you are my birthplace just the same.
Divided city of the green and blue
I look for her in you, my constant aim
to find a ghost within a close who speaks
in Highland Gaelic.
                              The bulldozer breaks

raw bricks to powder. Boyish workmen hang
like sailors in tall rigging. Buildings sail
into the future. The old songs you sang
fade in their pop songs, scale on dizzying scale.

All Our Ancestors

All our ancestors have gone abroad.
Their boots have other suns on them. They died
in Canada and Africa with God,

their mouths tasting of exile and of spray.
But you remained. Your grave is in Argyll
among the daffodils beside a tree

feathery and green. A stream runs by,
varying and oral, and your will
becomes a part of it, as the azure sky

trembles within it, not Canadian but
the brilliant sparklings of pure Highland light.

Of the Uncomplicated Dairy Girl

Of the uncomplicated dairy girl
in gown that's striped in blue and red
feeding the hens in a windy spring
by the green wooden shed
where shade after quick shade
endlessly shuttles let me speak
and speak unsorrowing.

As in the weather of a Lewis loom
a pastoral picture, striped against the blue,
against the stone, against the green,
against the cottage with its daisies
taking the place of roses
casting a meal from a young hand
still without its ring.

The long dress billows in the breeze
mixed like the confectionery
you'd bring home from the fishing
in the large yellow chest with hats,
silken things and coats,
just before your straight-backed brother
marched off to save the King.

Just stay there therefore for a moment,
uncomplicated dairy girl,
in your chequered screen of red and blue
holding the pail in your hand
before the sky is red and mooned
and feathered by (beyond the dance)
the beat of metal wings.

At the Scott Exhibition, Edinburgh Festival

(I)

He will outlast us, churning out his books,
advocate and historian, his prose
earning him Abbotsford with its borrowed gates,
its cheap mementos from the land he made.
Walking the room together in this merciless
galaxy of manuscripts and notes
I am exhausted by such energy.
I hold your hand for guidance. Over your brow

the green light falls from tall and narrow windows.
His style is ignorant of this tenderness,
the vulnerable angle of your body
below the Raeburn with its steady gaze.

(II)

It was all in his life, not in his books
"Oh I am dying, take me home to Scotland
where I can breathe though that breath were my last."
He limped through an Edinburgh being made anew.
He worked his way through debts, past a dead wife.
My dear, we love each other in our weakness
as he with white grave face diminishing through
stroke after stroke down to the unpaid room.
We know what we are but know not what we will be.
I tremble in this factory of books.
What love he must have lost to write so much.

In the Dark

Feeling across a field in the dark
one shields one's eyes against the wire fences.
The body tenses and the eye winces,
the feet feeling for ditches draw back.

And we remember that all our art
is dependent first on light and then on skill,
for how could any poet go to school
in a black field with such a checked stride?

Inching sometimes over unsteady stone
and by a black stream waiting, hearing its noise
and guessing from its small or major voice
how deep it is, how shallow, how serene,

aching intently for magnanimous light
which is the page and the reason for the page
the space which tempts us out to voyage
beyond the field, beyond its fenced limit.

The Glass of Water

My hand is blazing on the cold tumbler.
My eye looks through it to the other side.
If it were what is real, if it were heaven
how I corrupt it with my worn flesh.
How its neutrality is aggrandised
by fever and by empire. I constrain
and grasp this parish which is pastoral.

To be pure is not difficult, it's impossible.
How could the saint work to this poverty,
this unassumingness, this transparency?
How could his levels be so wholly calm?
The fact of water is unteachable.
It's less and more than honour standing up
invulnerable in its vulnerable glass.

Orpheus

(1)

And he said, I am come in search of her
bringing my single bitter gift. I have
nothing more precious to offer
than this salt venom seeming to you as love.
It is true I cannot live without her
since I am now shade who was once fire.
See, mineral spirit, how I now suffer
by the slow heavy motion of my lyre.

And the god then replying, Let her stay
for by her absence your music is more clear
barer and purer. Always in the air
her distance will perfect her as Idea.
Better the far sun of an April day
than fleshly thunder in the atmosphere.

(2)

And he said, That is great condemnation,
to live profoundly and yet much alone.
To see deeply by a barren passion.
It was forgetfully I moved the stone
which now submits to my examination.
She was my sense; around her flowing gown
my poems gathered in their proper season.
They were her harvest yet they were my own.

And the god then replying, What you say
is what her absence taught you. Our return
is not permissible to an earlier way.
If it were possible you would learn to mourn
even more deeply. Do you never burn
poems whose language was becoming gray?

(3)

And he to the god, If you should let her go
I'd know my music had its former power
to melt you too as once it melted snow
to alter you as once it altered her
so that in music we both learned to grow.
It was a dance of earth and of the air.
But up above it's easier. Here below —
The shade then smiled and said, Behold her there,

and he beheld her whitely where she stood
in that deep shade. She seemed not to have changed
nor he to have changed either as he played.

And yet her apparition was so strange.
She didn't fit the music that he made.
The notes and she were mutually disarranged.

(4)

And the god to him, Now I must tell you clear
what you refuse to see, since it is hard
to accuse ourselves of cruelty and fear.
You wished that she should die. And what you heard
was not my voice but yours condemning her.
If you will learn to love you must go forward.
For that is how it is in the upper air.
All that you have shared you have now shared.

And Orpheus took his lyre and left that place
and moved where the shadows moved and the clouds flowed
and all that had its own changing grace.
As on an April day there was sun and shade
but nothing vicious or virtuous
haunted the various music that he played.

Chinese Poem

(1)

To Seumas Macdonald,
                    now resident in Edinburgh —
I am alone here, sacked from the Department
for alcoholic practices and disrespect.
A cold wind blows from Ben Cruachan.
There is nothing here but sheep and large boulders.
Do you remember the nights with *Reliquae Celticae*
and those odd translations by Calder?
Buzzards rest on the wires. There are many seagulls.
My trousers grow used to the dung.

What news from the frontier? Is Donald still Colonel?
Are there more pupils than teachers in Scotland?
I send you this by a small boy with a pointed head.
Don't trust him. He is a Campbell.

(2)

The dog brought your letter today
from the red postbox on the stone gate
two miles away and a bit.
I read it carefully with tears in my eyes.
At night the moon is high over Cladach
and the big mansions of prosperous Englishmen.
I drank a half bottle thinking of Meg
and the involved affairs of Scotland.
When shall we two meet again
in thunder, lightning or in rain?
The carrots and turnips are healthy,
the *Farmers' Weekly* garrulous.
Please send me a *Radio Times* and a book
on cracking codes. I have much sorrow.
Mrs Macleod has a blue lion on her pants.
They make a queenly swish in a high wind.

(3)

There is a man here who has been building a house
for twenty years and a day.
He has a barrow in which he carries large stones.
He wears a canvas jacket.
I think I am going out of my mind.
When shall I see the city again,
its high towers and insurance offices,
its glare of unprincipled glass?
The hens peck at the grain.
The wind brings me pictures of exiles,
ghosts in tackety boots, lies,
adulteries in cornfields and draughty cottages.

91

I hear Donald is a brigadier now
and that there is fighting on the frontier.
The newspapers arrive late with strange signs on them.
I go out and watch the road.

(4)

Today I read five books.
I watched Macleod weaving a fence
to keep the eagles from his potatoes.
A dull horse is cobwebbed in rain.
When shall our land consider itself safe
from the assurance of the third rate mind?
We lack I think nervous intelligence.
Tell them I shall serve in any capacity,
a field officer, even a private,
so long as I can see the future
through uncracked field glasses.

(5)

A woman arrived today
in a brown coat and a brown muff.
She says we are losing the war,
that the Emperor's troops are everywhere
in their blue armour and blue gloves.
She says there are men in a stupor
in the ditches among the marigolds
crying "Alas, alas."
I refuse to believe her.
She is, I think, an agent provocateur.
She pretends to breed thistles.

92

from *The Notebooks of Robinson Crusoe*

(11)

The wind blows in my chimney. How mournful it is! I can
hear in it voices of exhortation, of warning, and of regret.

They speak of partings, wrecks and exile. They remind of
crimes inflicted on others and on oneself.

O that I were a man without memory, a machine renewed
by the days, a tree that forgets its autumn leaves, its winter
dispossessions.

O that like a cock I could crow in the morning, my red
hackles duplicating the sun's rays, my head fierce and
singular, my brassy extended throat dispersing the rack of
clouds.

(12)

Last night I drank much rum. I dreamed that you were in
my arms. Later I talked without ceasing.

Waking from my dishevelled bed, I entered a world so tidy
that I wept as you wept. If I had my mother's clock, with the
two Dutch figures, I would stay in the dark to watch you
step out in your green sabots.

But you are not there, the climate is constant, and the only
speaker is Pretty Poll who speaks beady eyed and without
humour the words, "Crusoe . . . Cruise . . . Crew," from the
world of his squalor, riffling his feathers, regarding me
from his red cage as I walk by the ruffled sea.

(14)

LANDSCAPE

This landscape is my diary.
I inscribe the day on it.
I invest it with grammar.
The rack of rocks I compose
in the blowing wind.

93

I say, "That apple tree
reminds me of someone.
I hang my ghosts on it,
hairily entering the sea."

(17)

In my leafed chapel I pray to God.
I say to myself: I am better than spastics, idiots, physically
ruined men.
I do not have TB, cancer, heart disease, or any plague.
My heart, lungs, kidneys, liver are sound.
I do not suffer the tremors of the bank clerk or the tempests
of the manager.
I do not pace up and down in a hospital waiting for the
doctor to tell me about my wife and whether the haemor-
rhages have stopped.
I do not hear the crazy white-haired violinist scraping in
the attic.
I am not feverish with love.
I do not phone my sweetheart at midnight from a squalid
bar, nor do I see her raising her shadowy lips to her lover's,
behind a closed curtain.
I do not stand by a stretcher watching the pale mouth
hardly breathing.
I do not see my children returning from the arena beaten.
I do not stand before the blank wall of my disabilities.
For all these things I give thanks to God.
Why then am I not happy?

(19)

Last night I saw in the moonlight standing by a tree Jim
Merrick whose last biscuit I ate on a raft in the Indian Ocean
just before he died. His bearded face vibrated like the rings
of the tree and then changed into seaweed pulsating with
miniature fish.

I stayed by my hut, my bones rattling like dice in a cup,
my sleepless lidless eyes steadily dilating.

Later by the candle, my breast heated by rum, I heard a bell ring distinct and near.

How much of the Bible I read I cannot remember nor how many souls betrayed, insatiable, writhed on the capsizing walls till dawn.

(21)

March and the world is white again
like notepaper, like a newspaper.
I could write a letter
of the plainest marble.
The wind goes over and over.
I am a fictional character
in the white newspaper.
Someone on a liner
is reading me.

(24)

I shall clamp my teeth.
I shall not bleed language.
If my condition is absurd let it be so.

Let me be steel. Irony's not enough.
I shall go down into my grave
below these foreign blooms.

Starlight dangles towards me. Let me wave
my handkerchief to the universe.
This is no place for rage.

I am the parrot of a lost routine.
I have a splendid cage
central to this green.

This is a comic place.
I shall carve my name on the trees
over and over.

It is possible that I shall grow used to this as a knot to wood and that, were rescuers brisk with pity and self congratulation, to emerge from the sea I should hide in the woods and like an animal peer at them fearfully between the slats of leaves.

It is possible that, aware of my kingship here, I would not return to anonymity there but that, breeding hauteur in my solitude, I should recoil from the momentary and dramatic solicitude of others.

For the oyster in the depths of the sea has its pearl as I my arrogance and, constant to my own sufficiency, I would disdain the million wandering fish sliding past, each on his own level.

It is possible that, my own god worshipping my own images, I would not wish to enter, unshaven and hairy, the monotonous climate of the mediocre, but would prefer my extreme pain to their temperate ordinariness.

O Lord, let me know my mortality: let me cast myself on the common waters. Let me be resurrected by the cheap tarnished glorious tinfoil light.

(28)

NAMES

I

Noon: and the gluttonous ocean sparkles. I know that it can drown me, that its fish can fine me down to bone. I know the capabilities of its factory.
Nevertheless how can I nail my 'sea' to sea, my 'hill' to hill. And how can my 'well' furnish me with water?

II

And how can my 'ought' emerge from this summer? From its multiplicity of leaves, its unknown flowers, its whirr of ignorant insects.
How can the data erect a ladder? How can the immigrant lay down his rules?

How can the green shade breed its commandments? Or the snake, with its typical hissing, sway its small head against mine?

III

I walk about, egotist of the day, yet the beast bird and insect have their own concerns, are enveloped in their own armour. My philosophy is the excess of leisure, my religion the questionings of idleness.
Yet to exist is to be vain: to move is to be noticed.
The snake rears itself like a question, interrogating eternity.

(30)

Island, what shall I say of you, your peat bogs, your lochs, your moors and berries?
The cry of your birds in the fading evening.
Your flowers in summer glowing brightly where there are no thoroughfares.
The perpetual sound of the sea.
The spongy moss on which feet imprint themselves.
The mountains which darken and brighten like ideas in the mind.
The owl with its big glasses that perch on a late tree listening.
The mussels clamped to the rocks, the fool's gold, the tidal pools filling and emptying.
The corn that turns from pale green to yellow, my scarecrow rattling in the wind.
The smoke that arises from my fire.

This I say:
One man cannot warm the world.
This I say:
The world of one man is different from the world of many men.

This I say:
Without the net, the sweetest fish are tasteless.

97

(33)

When they rescue me I shall return to the perfumed vaude-
villes and machinery, to the music halls of the fat sopranos,
to the Master of Ceremonies with the tucked tails, the
moustache, the stick and the voluminous words. I shall see
the advertisements which illuminate the sky, our homes of
Viyella, Vibroso and Vitamins.

I shall leave my bare island, simple as poison, to enter the
equally poisonous world of Tiberius, where there are echoes
and reflections, a Hall of Mirrors in which my face like all
faces swells like a jester's in a world without sense.

(34)

I have read them all, Sartre, Wittgenstein, Ryle. I have
listened at midday to the actresses popstars authors in
"Desert Island Discs" speculating happily on islands among
the traffic of London (Am I allowed dettol and bandages?
Voltaire?)
And as I remember hell, the choice of staying by the
communal inferno where we feed on each other or going
alone into the middle of the dark wood leaving behind me
forever the Pickwicks and the iced candles of Christmas, I
hear now clearly in the hollow spaces of the valleys, in the
roar of the waterfall, in the appearance of the birds of spring
and their departure in the autumn the same phrase repeated
over and over:

Language is other people.

(41)

It is not with sorrow that I stand on deck and leave behind
me the island and the thirty years of my life there.
It is rather with puzzlement as if a dream were beginning
again, the dream of officers in white, seamen in blue, tele-
vision cameras, the manic unblinking eye of the announcer.
The enigma of the dream persists as the jovial captain at the
head of yards of white linen quizzes me, between draughts
of wine: as the sailors weave about me their human erotic
legends!

As the ship steadily steers towards the cameras providing
rich merchandise for my new dream and I emerge from the
world of sparse iron into the vast cinema of sensation.

When Day is Done

Sorrow remembers us when day is done.
It sits in its old chair gently rocking
and singing tenderly in the evening.
It welcomes us home again after the day.
It is so old in its black silken dress,
its stick beside it carved with legends.
It tells its stories over and over again.
After a while we have to stop listening.

The Chair

The tall green-backed chair
in a room with brown walls
and all the old questions
start here.

If I had met you elsewhere
if you had dried your tears
with a different handkerchief
in a different hand —

and the tall green-backed chair
seems so fixed and solid
like a family lawyer
in all the thunderstorms.

My Child

My child, where are you?
The woods are waning
and I am seeking you among the hedges.

I am still wearing my stiff gown
which often sustained you
among the stones and thistles.

I bring you the right shape of things.
I bring you the warm bread
with the crust on it.

I bring you the bottles
with the white milk in them,
the knives and the spoons.

I bring you our house with the rigid roof on it,
the cupboards with their groceries,
the wardrobes with your ironed clothes.

I bring you the made bed,
the fire with the red voice,
the rectangular windows.

Child, I am looking for you.

They tell me you are in the rivers
growing haphazardly
dabbled in water.

My voice comes to you across the cornstacks,
across my completed harvest,
across the sharp stubble.

Women

Bewildered and angry is the sap of women
as if the tree were to fight against itself
in a hurt greenness, in a swaying current,
in a wrestle to put out flowers or thorns.

Man often strolls down an avenue of ideas,
his hands in his pockets cool and lenient.
It is the morning for a cigarette
or for a joke from his worn pack of cards.

Woman sees no humour in the sky.
Earth is a purse which feeds us.
The tidied child is heading towards marriage
and then a fixed place in the earth,

or perhaps in astrology, that favoured village,
which sheds names sensibly and certainly.
The girl walks in the steps of Pisces,
in the chains of Virgo, in its green lanes.

Man measures the stars' heat and incidence,
their probability, their constituents.
Their naval and other councils are formal.
Their disentangled language is of weather.

Women follow the moon down yellow pages,
their bodies shaken by winds, teeth chattering.
Their roots whine and sing. They grip their acre.
Sometimes they float out on eerie tides.

Tears are Salt

Tears are salt like the sea.
How reality breaks in on us
while we are acting so well
on our tiny stages,

dressed up so sunnily
wearing our brooches and belts
considering the world
as just about our size.

Suddenly reality is there
with its large crude torch
shining it into our eyes
and into our guts.

The sunbeam just passing
is carrying a coffin
as a bee will carry pollen
home to its hive.

In the centre of the tear
is a small inverted man
gazing down at the sky
and a pair of dusty shoes.

Tears are salt like the sea.
Standing together
we look out from the headland
at a mouth burbling with foam.

None is the Same as Another

None is the same as another,
O none is the same.

That none is the same as another
is a matter for crying
since never again will you see
that one, once gone.

In their brown hoods
the pilgrims are crossing the land
and many will look the same
but all are different

and their ideas fly to them
on accidental winds
perching awhile in their minds
from different valleys.

None is the same as another,
O none is the same.

And that none is the same is not
a matter for crying.

Stranger, I take your hand,
O changing stranger.

The Iolaire

The green washed over them. I saw them when
the New Year brought them home. It was a day
that orbed the horizon with an enigma.
It seemed that there were masts. It seemed that men
buzzed in the water round them. It seemed that fire
shone in the water which was thin and white
unravelling towards the shore. It seemed that I
touched my fixed hat which seemed to float and then
the sun illumined fish and naval caps,
names of the vanished ships. In sloppy waves,
in the fat of water, they came floating home
bruising against their island. It is true
a minor error can inflict this death,
that star is not responsible. It shone

over the puffy blouse, the flapping blue
trousers, the black boots. The seagulls swam
bonded to the water. Why not man?
The lights were lit last night, the tables creaked
with hoarded food. They willed the ship to port
in the New Year which would erase the old,
its errant voices, its unpractised tones.
Have we done ill, I ask? My sober hat
floated in the water, my fixed body
a simulacrum of the transient waste,
for everything was mobile, planks that swayed,
the keeling ship exploding, and the splayed
cold insect bodies. I have seen your church
solid. This is not. The water pours
into the parting timbers where I ache
above the globular eyes. The slack heads turn
ringing the horizon without a sound
with mortal bells, a strange exuberant flower
unknown to our dry churchyards. I look up.
The sky begins to brighten as before,
remorseless amber, and the bruised blue grows
at the erupting edges. I have known you, God,
not as the playful one but as the black
thunderer from hills. I kneel
and touch this dumb blonde head. My hand is scorched.
Its human quality confuses me.
I have not felt such hair so dear before
nor seen such real eyes. I kneel from you.
This water soaks me. I am running with
its tart sharp joy. I am floating here.
In my black uniform, I am embraced
by these green ignorant waters. I am calm.

Autumn

Autumn again. A wide-eyed absence in
the woods and skies. The trees, once berry-ripe,
are cleared of weight and in the midday shine

forlorn, perhaps. Triumphant. It is true
that exile, parting, is our earthly lot
though roots cling tight below the green and blue.
O handkerchiefs wave free while the full heart
is squeezed of purple leaving the wrinkled skin.
Depend on everything depend on art,
your crystal table set with paper, pen,
such simple instruments. Begin once more.
Spring in its fury breaks on us again
frizzle of summer, winter with its snow,
and also autumn — beating the hazels down
from trees enriched by taste and by red hue.

Art feeds us, famished. It's the heavenly crown,
the earthly crown against the distant blue.

My Brother

My brother, today the rain is falling,
I haven't heard from you for twenty years.
When you left first you were so confident,
riding your new horse from coast to coast.
Then after a while you stopped writing.
My letters never reached you for you changed addresses.
Were you ashamed that your new horse never lasted?
Sailors from the old country have seen you in bars
but you don't speak to them.
Success is demanded of the exile.
Today as the rain falls it occurred to me

that I do not know where you are.
How the world comes between even two brothers!
All I can see is the horse you wrote of
standing in a cage of rain somewhere
with the burrs of twenty years on its skin.

Remembering

When the wind blows the curtains wide, do you not remember
the green trams on their wires and yourself young,
singing on a street that no one now can find.
It is as if the book opens, showing the parts you have played
in a theatre more precious to you than The Globe
with its ghostly flags flying in an Elizabethan wind.

Next Time

Listen, when you come home
to see your wife again
where the tapestry stands unfinished
across the green brine,
sit among the stones
and consider how it was
in the old days
before you became a king
and walked hunchbacked
with decisions on your shoulders.

Sit among the rocks
hearing the sound of the sea
eternally unchanging
and watch the butter-cups
so luminously pale.

The cries of the dead
haunt the gaunt headland
and the shields clash
in that astonishing blue.

Simply enter the boat
and leave the island
for there is no return,
boy, forerunner of kings.

Next time, do this,
salt bronzed veteran
let the tapestry be unfinished
as truthful fiction is.

Returning Exile

Home he came after Canada
Where for many years he drank
his failure into the ground.
Westward lay Lewis. He never wrote.
The snow needs a gay pen.
However at the age of fifty-five
he put on his hat, his painted tie,
and packed his trunk, being just alive.
Quietly he sailed over waters
through which he saw his home all green
and salmon leaping between deer's horns.
Arrived home he attended church,
the watch-chain snaking his waistcoat.
No one was as black or stiff as he.
He cast his bottles into outer darkness
where someone gnashed his teeth
each evening by the quay
watching the great ship sail out

with the girls laughing
the crew in white
and the bar mazy with mirrors.
Some called her SS. Remorse,
others the bad ship Envy.

The Exiles
(translated from the author's own Gaelic)

The many ships that left our country
with white wings for Canada.
They are like handkerchiefs in our memories
and the brine like tears
and in their masts sailors singing
like birds on branches.
That sea of May running in such blue,
a moon at night, a sun at daytime,
and the moon like a yellow fruit,
like a plate on a wall
to which they raise their hands
like a silver magnet
with piercing rays
streaming into the heart.

Australia

1

In Australia the trees are deathly white,
the kangaroos are leaping halfway to heaven
but land at last easily on the earth.
Sometimes I hear graves singing
their Gaelic songs to the dingos

which scrabble furiously at the clay.
Then tenderly in white they come towards me,
drifting in white, the far exiles
buried in the heart of brown deserts.
It is a strange language they speak
not Australian not Gaelic
while the green eyes stalk them
under a moon the same as ours
but different, different.

2

Naturally there are photographs of Ned Kelly
in his iron mask in his iron armour.
His iron body hung stiffly in the wind
which blew past the ravens.
In that dry land his armour will not rust
and the hot sun flashes from it
as if it were a mirror, creator of fresh stars.
However dingos leap at it they will not chew him
for he is a story, a poem,
a tale that is heard on the wind.

3

No, you will not return from Australia
however you may wish to do so.
For you have surrendered to its legend,
to its music being continually reborn,
to the eerie whine of its deserts.
Somehow or another it entered your soul
and however much you remember Scotland,
its graves sanctified by God,
its historical darknesses,
you will not return from it.
Its dust is in your nostrils,
its tenderness has no justice,
its millions of stars are the thoughts
of unbridled horsemen.

With blue eyes you will stare
blinded into its blueness
and when you remember your rivers,
the graveyards the mountains,
it is Australia that stands up in front of you,
your question, your love.

4

All day the kookaburra is laughing
from the phantoms of trees,
from the satire of nature.
It is not tragedy nor comedy,
it is the echo of beasts,
the bitter chorus of thorns,
and flowers that have names
that aren't easily remembered.
The kookaburra laughs from the trees,
from the branches of ghosts,
but the sky remains blue
and the eyes glow green in the night.

No Return

No, really you can't go back to
that island any more. The people
are growing more and more unlike you
and the fairy stories
have gone down to the grave in peace.

The wells are dry now and the long grasses
parched by their mouths, and the horned cows
have gone away to another country
where someone else's imagination
is fed daily on milk.

There were, you remember, sunsets
against which the black crows were seen
and a moonlight of astonishing beauty
calmed at midnight by waters
which you're not able to hear.

The old story-telling people
have gone home to their last houses
under the acres of a lost music.
These have all been sold now
to suave strangers with soft voices.

It is a great pity that your cottage
preserved in January by clear ice
and in June surrounded by daisies
has been sold to the same strangers
and the bent witches evicted.

If you were to return now the roofs
would appear lower, the walls would have no echoes,
the wavelike motion would be lost,
the attics where you read all day
would be crammed with antiques.

No, you cannot return to an island
expecting that the dances will be unchanged,
that the currency won't have altered,
that the mountains blue in the evening
will always remain so.

You can't dip your mouth in the pure spring
ever again or ever again be haunted
by the 'eternal sound of the ocean'.
Even the boats which you once rowed
have set off elsewhere.

The witches wizards harlequins jesters
have packed up their furniture and guitars.
The witches have gone home on their broomsticks
and the conjurors with their small horses
and tiny carts have departed

leaving the island bare, bleak and windy,
itself alone in its barren corner
composed of real rocks and real flowers
indifferent to the rumours and the stories
stony, persistent.

Reading Shakespeare

On a dark day in winter I read Shakespeare.
The birds set off to branches of the south.
I tremble in the branches of the mind.

Summer is finished. Shakespeare always remains,
tree on tree for ever fragrant, young,
leaves that never fall out of the leaves.

Forest of Arden, you are my best south,
the lightning wit in this locality,
the cloudless sky, the rainbow tunics there,

and thunder too. We have the best of it,
so many weathers, changeable, intense.
Farewell to the long-necked geese that cross the sea.

Speech for Prospero

When I left that island I thought I was dead. Nothing
stirred in me. Miranda in jeans
and totally innocent was standing by a sail
and all the others happily recovered talking
in suits made of brine. But to return to
the gossip, the poisonous ring, was not easy,
and many times I nearly tried to turn back
feeling in my bones the desolate hum of the headland,
my creation of rivers and mist.
Still we went on. The corruption had put on flesh,
the young were hopeful again, all was forgiven.
Nevertheless the waiters were scraping and bowing,
the rumours beginning, the crowns of pure crystal were sparkling,
the telephones were ringing with messages from the grave
and the thin phosphorescent boys glowing with ambition
in corners of velvet and death.
Still I went on. The ship left its wake behind it,
shining and fading, cord of a new birth,
and over the rail Miranda gazed at her prince
yearning for love.
Goodbye, island, never again shall I see you,
you are part of my past. Though I may dream of you often
I know there's a future we all must learn to accept,
music working itself out in the absurd halls and the mirrors,
posturings of men like birds, Art in a torrent of plates,
the sound of the North Wind, distant yet close,
as stairs ascend from the sea.

"You'll take a bath"

"And now you'll take a bath," she'd always say,
just when I was leaving, to keep me back.
At the second turning of the stony stair
the graffiti were black letters in a book
misspelt and menacing. As I drove away
she'd wave from the window. How could I always bear
to be her knight abandoning her to her tower
each second Sunday, a ghost that was locked fast
in a Council scheme, where radios played all day
unknown raw music, and young couples brought
friends home to midnight parties, and each flower
in the grudging garden died in trampled clay.

Standing by her headstone in the mild
city of bell-less doors, I feel the sweat
stink my fresh shirt out, as each gravelly path
becomes a road, long lost, in a bad bet.
Once more I see the dirty sleepy child.
"The water's hot enough. You'll have a bath."

And almost I am clean but for that door
so blank and strong, imprinted with her name
as that far other in the scheme was once,
and 'scheme' becomes a mockery, and a shame,
in this neat place, where each vase has its flower,
and the arching willow its maternal stance.

Breughel

A bony horse with a bird on it droops its head.
With a cart of skulls like potatoes Death drives onward.

There's a storm of monsters, snouted and obscene,
and on another page a neat snow scene.

Large peasants dance under a leaden sky
and ships are sinking in a black-framed sea.

The blind raise tortured faces. In Cockayne
they eat and drink and sleep and at the moon

a peasant pisses. Proverbs multiply.
Children with adult faces gravely play

while aprons break the storm, red plates and jugs,
Death in a hood and lands pulled back like rugs.

And over the countryside the black birds go
with far below them hunters in the snow.

Owl and Mouse

The owl wafts home with a mouse in its beak.
The moon is stunningly bright in the high sky.

Such a gold stone, such a brilliant hard light.
Such large round eyes of the owl among the trees.

All seems immortal but for the dangling mouse,
an old hurt string among the harmony

of the masterful and jewelled orchestra
which shows no waste soundlessly playing on.

For Poets Writing in English over in Ireland

"Feeling," they said,
"that's the important thing"—
those poets who write in English over in Ireland.

It was late.
There was dancing in the hall,
playing of pipes, of bones, of the penny whistle.

They were an island in that Irishness.
"Larkin and Dunn," they said. "Now Dunn is open
to more of the world than ageing Larkin is.

What room was Mr Bleaney in? It's like
going to any tenement and finding
any name you can think of on the door.

And you wonder a little about him but not much."
We were sitting on the floor outside the room
where a song in Irish waltzed the Irish round.

Do the stones, the sea, seem different in Irish?
Do we walk in language, in a garment pure
as water? Or as earth just as impure?

The grave of Yeats in Sligo, Innisfree
island seen shivering on an April day.
The nuns who cycle down an Easter road.

The days are beads strung on a thin wire.
Language at Connemara is stone
and the water green as hills is running westwards.

The little children in the primary school
giggling at little at our Scottish Gaelic,
writing in chalk the Irish word for 'knife'.

To enter a different room. When did Bleaney
dance to the bones? This world is another world.
A world of a different language is a world

we find our way about in with a stick,
half-deaf half-blind, snatching a half word there,
seeing a twisted figure in a mirror,

slightly unnerved, unsure. I must go home.
To English? Gaelic? O beautiful Maud Gonne,
the belling hounds spoke in what language to you?

In that tall tower so finished and so clear
his international name was on the door
and who would ask who had been there before him?

I turn a page and read an Irish poem
translated into English and it says
(the poet writing of his wife who'd died):

"Half of my eyes you were, half of my hearing,
half of my walking you were, half of my side."
From what strange well are these strange words upspringing?

But then I see you, Yeats, inflexible will,
creator of yourself, a conscious lord,
writing in English of your own Maud Gonne.

Inside the room there's singing and there's dancing.
Another world is echoing with its own
music that's distant from the world of Larkin.

And I gaze at the three poets. They are me,
poised between two languages. They have chosen
with youth's superb confidence and decision.

"Half of my side you were, half of my seeing,
half of my walking you were, half of my hearing."
Half of this world I am, half of this dancing.

Halloween

Someone was playing the piano when quite suddenly
there they were standing in the room.
They would not sing or speak or tell their names.
Their skull faces blankly shifted round
as if they were studying us implacably.
"Yokels," one said. "Rustics," said another,
and truly they had come in out of the rain
with their masks tall and white and bony-looking.
"Macbeth," someone said, and someone, "Hamlet".
Or perhaps at least the 'Elegy' by Gray.
The rain drummed on the roof and they were gone
in their muddy boots, squelching past cowering doors.
We looked at each other. It was graveyard time
as our black ties on our white shirts might say.

The 'Ordinary' People

The 'ordinary' people sing on the edge of the grave.
When the hero howls and cries they are humming
in the middle of ropes, griefs, the deaths of roses.

The 'ordinary' people are not stones.
They are revengeful, bitter, quick to strike and laugh
and they buy oranges at the market-place.

The 'ordinary' people say, "I'll not be put upon."
They spend their money freely on food and drink
and then they have no money, only hope.

Where does the hope come from that they see,
who live precariously by the deaths of roses,
and hang their washing among tragedies?

I begin to think there are no 'ordinary' people.

Or rather that they've learned about tragedies
from birth and can simply pass them by
or walk through them clutching food, bottles.

I believe there is no such thing as tragedy,
that the hero has deceived us, is the red infant
howling and screaming from his wooden cage.

At the Funeral of Robert Garioch

Something about the April day
touched me
as they slid your coffin onto the trolley
in the Crematorium.

More and more often it troubles me
this wind my sails have missed
which is still around me
fluttering the bluebells.

"The Lord's My Shepherd" we sang.
It was time for the burning.
The minister blessed it
dressed in his white gown,

his voice fat and voluptuous,
his enunciation pure.
You slid down into fire
in your yellow coffin.

In half-way April
the breeze was vulnerable
straying among the warble
of the first birds.

Poet, the flowers open
even when we are dead
even when the power has gone
from our right arms.

The flowers open in flame.
The coffin slides home.
Fugitive April becomes
a tremendous summer.

Who Daily

Who daily at the rickety table
writes and sings, writes and sings,
Venus with the one arm,
Apollo with the one leg,
the stuttering rainbow that hirples
like early crayons into the sea.

Envoi

There are
more things in heaven and earth, Horatio,
than bones, roses. There are windows
through which gaunt faces peer
and there are children
running through great doors.

Consider
how the sea roars mournfully at the edge of
all things, how the seaweed
hangs at the sailor's neck, the crab
shuffles in armour, Horatio,
the punctual dead visit us, rise
bird-voiced from the grass,
and the owls
are scholars of the woods.
Horatio, I remember
a kingdom and a kingdom's diplomat,
a girl floating tenderly down stream,
a crown on her young head.
These are portents, warnings, ominous
reflections from the mirror.
Horatio
my eyes darken. Tragedy is
nothing but a churned foam.
I wave to you
from this secure and leafy entrance,
this wooden
door on which I bump my head,
this moment and then,
that.